In Memory Of

Scott Petersen 1983

Dedicated by the
Carleton College
Alumni Association

Self-Identity
and Human Happiness

american
university
studies

Series V
Philosophy

Vol. 198

PETER LANG
New York • Washington, D.C./Baltimore • Bern
Frankfurt am Main • Berlin • Brussels • Vienna • Oxford

Michael Dahlem

Self-Identity and Human Happiness

PETER LANG
New York • Washington, D.C./Baltimore • Bern
Frankfurt am Main • Berlin • Brussels • Vienna • Oxford

Library of Congress Cataloging-in-Publication Data

Dahlem, Michael W.
Self-identity and human happiness / Michael Dahlem.
p. cm. — (American university studies. V, Philosophy; vol. 198)
Includes bibliographical references.
1. Happiness. 2. Self. 3. Happiness—Social aspects. 4. Social justice.
I. Title. II. Series: American university studies.
Series V, Philosophy; v. 198.
BJ1481.D34 170—dc22 2005016046
ISBN 0-8204-7935-7
ISSN 0739-6392

Bibliographic information published by **Die Deutsche Bibliothek**.
Die Deutsche Bibliothek lists this publication in the "Deutsche
Nationalbibliografie"; detailed bibliographic data is available
on the Internet at http://dnb.ddb.de/.

The paper in this book meets the guidelines for permanence and durability
of the Committee on Production Guidelines for Book Longevity
of the Council of Library Resources.

© 2005 Peter Lang Publishing, Inc., New York
275 Seventh Avenue, 28th Floor, New York, NY 10001
www.peterlangusa.com

Printed in Germany

To Linda

Table of Contents

Acknowledgments ix

Introduction 1

Chapter 1. The Divided Self 9

Chapter 2. The Death Instinct 21

Chapter 3. The Right and the Good 37

Chapter 4. The Priority of Liberty 57

Chapter 5. Self-Identity and Species Being 71

Chapter 6. The Universal Self 85

Chapter 7. The Just Society 101

Notes 109

Bibliography 123

Acknowledgments

I would like to thank the following individuals for their thoughtful commentary and general assistance in the development of this project: Ron Perrin, Phil Fandozzi, Mary Gibson, Doug Husak, Howard McGarry, Fred McGlynn, Jim Pope, Jim Todd and Ted Solomon.

Introduction

According to the Big Bang Theory, the entire universe has exploded into existence from a single point of infinite density. If the physical universe has developed from what Stephen Hawking and others have called a "singularity," then so too have the minds necessary to comprehend the universe. This simple observation, which suggests that all beings share a common origin and a common identity, is the central idea that will guide this study of self-identity and human happiness.

Happiness has been a perennial concern of philosophy. Plato and Aristotle believed that happiness represents the proper final end for mankind. Classical utilitarians held that it constitutes the only thing good in itself. Even the Christian philosophy of the middle ages and the moral philosophy of the eighteenth century, while emphasizing duty, offered the promise of happiness.

More recently, the philosopher Herbert Marcuse maintained that human happiness requires an order of abundance, self-knowledge and social justice. Abundance is necessary to satisfy our material needs; self-knowledge to overcome a death instinct inherent in consciousness; and social justice to permit the full development of our creative powers as free and equal beings.

Furthermore, the just society is the one that maximizes the values of individual liberty and social equality. Liberty is a fundamental human value because we need the freedom to pursue our own conceptions of the good life. Equality is a fundamental value because our self-esteem depends on the way we are regarded by others.

Any inquiry into the subject of human happiness requires an analysis of the self. Indeed, human history may be understood as the search for self-identity. In his dialogues, Plato described a tripartite self defined by reason, will and sensuousness. Karl Marx also described a divided self characterized by self-consciousness, creativity and a social nature. In his early work, Marx designated the self as a "species being" which appropriates nature in order to actualize itself. Class societies, however, have prevented us from realizing our identity as species beings. For that reason, he called for the abolition of class society as a prerequisite for self-actualization and human happiness.

In addition to the tripartite divisions described by Plato and Marx, the self may be described by a series of dualities such as subject and object, mind and body, male and female, and the one and the many. Harmonizing these divisions and dualities lies at the heart of this inquiry.

The identity of the self is far from clear. As the subject of consciousness, it is impossible to understand the self in the same way that we understand an object of consciousness. While we can experience, understand and remember sensations, ideas and emotions, we cannot directly experience, understand or remember the self that senses, conceives and feels. This qualitative difference explain why there is no generally accepted science of consciousness.

Nevertheless, few people would disagree with David Hume's observation that there is an apparent constancy to the self that persists through time. It is my belief that a conception of the self as an unchanging, universal subject of consciousness may explain Hume's observation. Such a conception may also explain the belief that I have a body rather than that I am a body.

Moreover, the idea of an unchanging, universal self may provide a philosophical justification for our commitment to the values of liberty and equality. As noted above, individual liberty is a fundamental value because, as the creator of value, we need the freedom to pursue our own conceptions of the good life. Social equality is fundamental because, as social beings with a common identity, self-respect requires the respect of others.

The realization of both liberty and equality has been a daunting task. The individual liberty made possible by a capitalist division of labor has been largely achieved at the expense of social equality while the social equality made possible by a socialist division of labor has resulted in a diminution of individual liberty. If social justice and human happiness require both liberty and equality, then neither corporate capitalism nor state socialism will provide the necessary institutional framework. Instead, it will be necessary to establish social institutions that satisfy basic human needs and preserve civil liberties by promoting technical innovation, social democracy and the rule of law. Indeed, nothing less than a fundamental reform of our social, political and economic institutions will bring about the happiness we seek.

This work is divided into seven chapters. Chapter 1 discusses the historic preoccupation of philosophy with human happiness, beginning with Plato's conception of the good as eternal beauty and his conception of happiness as the eternal possession of the good. According to Plato, one who possesses the good will want to keep it forever. This wish reveals a desire for immortality which can be satisfied, in part, through the generation of offspring or the production of great works. True immortality, however, is reserved for the otherworldly realm of forms.

In this chapter, I also trace the idea of a divided self in the works of Plato, Nietzsche, Freud, Marx and Marcuse. For Plato, this division finds expression in the repression of our emotions and appetites in favor of the rule of reason. This psychological hierarchy corresponds to the hierarchical division of labor described in his ideal republic.

Like Plato, Marx saw a divided self in class societies marked by a coercive division of labor. Unlike Plato, however, Marx did not view such division as necessary for the preservation of social order. Instead, he argued that the divided self could be healed through the abolition of capitalism and the creation of a social order that promoted the development of human abilities. Marx's call for social revolution was pursued by Marcuse in the development of his critical theory of society.

In chapter 2, I note that the repressive aspects of Plato's psychology were explored by Sigmund Freud in his metapsychological speculations. Freud posited the existence of a "death instinct" as the source of human aggressiveness. He described the instinct as an urge inherent in organic life to return to the peacefulness of inorganic existence and he held that social progress made the repression of the instinct inevitable. In describing instinctual repression in these terms, Freud rejected the Marxian claim that repression could be overcome with the abolition of class society.

In response to the analyses of Freud and Marx, Marcuse sought to demonstrate that a non-repressive civilization is theoretically possible. Marcuse adopted Freud's death instinct, but described the instinct not as a desire for death, but for the reduction of pain. He believed that as life became more pleasurable, death would cease to be an instinctual goal.

Marcuse also maintained that the death instinct has altered our use of reason. He asserted that instrumental reason has acquired a technological character in its service to the forces of social domination. He coined the term "technological rationality" to designate the use of reason that makes technical efficiency the goal of human action.

For Marcuse, technological rationality has made our relationship to nature one of mastery and domination. When applied to the study of human nature, technological rationality is employed to maintain a social order—not of liberty and equality—but of domination and servitude. This order threatens to sever the bond between reason and happiness because the purpose of the technical apparatus does not coincide with the goal of happiness.

In his search for an answer to technological rationality and social division,

Marcuse invoked Plato's conception of the good as eternal beauty. He argued that in authentic works of art there is a harmony between reason and sensuousness that can transform the structure of our needs. He saw the fulfillment of the need for aesthetic enjoyment in the abolition of domination and servitude. In this way, Marcuse believed that authentic art could shape the consciousness of the men and women for whom social change has become a vital need.

In the end, however, he concluded that the fact of death rules out the possibility of a lasting happiness. For Marcuse, the self remains divided between the finite being it is and the eternal being it seeks, but cannot attain. Despite this pessimistic conclusion, his commitment to social justice as a necessary condition for human happiness deserves careful scrutiny. Moreover, his call for the abolition of capitalism plays a key role in the analysis of competing theories of justice.

Chapter 3 examines teleological and deontological theories of justice. A teleological theory, such as Aristotle's perfectionism or Mill's utilitarianism, seeks to promote a particular end, such as virtue or happiness while a deontological theory emphasizes our duty to others as separate moral agents.

In this chapter, I reject the claim that deontological theories of justice are neutral with respect to conceptions of the good life. Instead, every definition of the right is derived from some conception of the good. I also contend that it is not the priority of the right which distinguishes deontological from teleological theories, but the priority of liberty over equality.

I further assert that the deontological emphasis on the separateness of persons provides an inadequate theoretical basis for the achievement of social justice and human happiness. Social equality is better supported by a conception of the self with a common identity.

Finally, I examine the competing claims of deontological and teleological theories with regard to the values of liberty and equality. While these values are central to both traditions, each conceives of them differently. Deontology views liberty as freedom from constraint while teleology sees it as freedom for the development of human abilities. These competing conceptions of liberty bear directly on the meaning of equality in each tradition.

Chapter 4 analyzes the priority of liberty at work in the deontological tradition, with an emphasis on John Rawls's theory of justice as fairness. I note that the contrasts between the teleological and deontological traditions are misleading because there are two versions of teleological theory. One version seeks to maximize the satisfaction of individual preferences while the other seeks to promote goods that are to everyone's advantage. While Rawls is correct to reject the former, his own theory of justice as fairness seeks to realize the latter.

On examination, Rawls's principles of justice follow from a "thin theory" of the good which hypothetical contractors adopt in what he called the "original position." Without knowing their social circumstances, Rawls claimed that contractors would endorse goods such as liberty and opportunity, income and wealth, and the social bases of self-respect no matter what else they might wish. These social primary goods form the basis for Rawls's two principles of justice: the principle of the greatest equal liberty and the difference principle. The latter requires an equal distribution of social goods except where an unequal distribution would benefit the least advantaged.

Because Rawls's principles of justice invoke a conception of the human good, his distinction between the teleology of the ancients and the deontology of the moderns turns not on the priority of the right or the good, but on the nature of the human good. Rawls's theory of justice as fairness is in accord with the determination of preference utilitarians that individuals should be the sole judge of their own happiness. But in contrast to preference utilitarianism, he made use of the liberal harm principle to impose constraints on individual preferences. In this regard, he shared with perfectionists the belief that not all desires are worthy of consideration. Justice as fairness, therefore, differs from perfectionism not with regard to the priority of the right, but with respect to the nature of the good to be promoted. While perfectionists endorse virtue, justice as fairness promotes liberty and equality.

In exploring the contrast between the deontological and teleological traditions, it is worth noting that human happiness has received relatively little attention in deontological theories of justice. In contrast to the ancient preoccupation with happiness as the proper end of mankind and with moral education as the responsibility of the state, deontological theories tie human happiness to the successful completion of individual life plans while declaring that the state must remain neutral with respect to the efficacy of such plans. In the liberal state, individuals are free to pursue any plan of life that does not violate the rights of others. In the process, happiness becomes a purely personal concern for individuals who share no agreement about the good life.

Human happiness may have received less attention in the deontological tradition because of an inadequate conception of the self. Critics of deontological liberalism have maintained that the conception of the self as an autonomous chooser of ends necessarily results in the elevation of liberty over equality because liberty is essential to the successful completion of every plan of life. In contrast, Marx's conception of the self as a species being reflects a commitment to equality as an essential confirmation of a common identity. In the end, both conceptions reveal a fundamental truth about human nature: we are both the creators of value and beings whose self-esteem depends on the way we are regarded by others.

Chapter 5 explores Marx's philosophical anthropology. Marx distinguished human beings from other animals on the basis of our self-consciousness, creativity and social nature. These features may be said to correspond to our reason, will and sensuousness or material being. He also held that, as rational creatures, we are conscious not only of our immediate surroundings, but of the relations between objects not present to our senses. Furthermore, self-consciousness means that we can understand our relationship with others as a confirmation of our species being.

Marx followed Nietzsche and others in holding that, as a creator of value, human beings have the power to actualize what exists only in the imagination. We also have the ability to recognize this power in others. Finally, our material being ensures our social nature. Not only are we indebted to others for our physical existence, but our material needs can be satisfied only in association with others.

In this chapter, I defend this philosophical anthropology from the claim that Marx was overly materialistic in emphasizing our capacity for creativity. Following Hegel, G.A. Cohen has argued that our search for self-identity requires a connection to something which the self has not created. Without disagreeing with this assertion, I attempt to show that Marx's conception of the self as a species being satisfies this need and provides a philosophical basis for the establishment of the true community necessary for the achievement of human happiness.

Chapter 6 expands upon Marx's conception of the self. While the Marxian conception provides a philosophical justification for the value of social equality that is lacking in deontological theories of justice, the conception of the self as a species being leaves unanswered our relationship to the rest of nature. To address this shortcoming, I argue for a broader conception of the self as a universal subject of consciousness. This conception finds support in the teachings of Eastern religions and the discoveries of Western physics as described in the works of Fritjof Capra, Deepak Chopra and Stephen Hawking.

At the core of this conception is the observation that the entire universe, including the laws of nature and the minds necessary to understand those laws, has emerged from a single point of infinite density. It is this point, referred to as a singularity by physicists and mathematicians, that constitutes the self that is both subject and object, mind and body, male and female, the one and the many.

The conception of a universal self has significant implications for political philosophy and social practice. It provides a justification for social equality while affirming the importance of individual liberty. It is in accord with our commitment to universal reason, the rational autonomy of the moral subject, and the promotion of the common good. In positing the existence of a divided self in search of unity, the conception of a universal self may explain the death instinct and the division of society into antagonistic classes while offering a guide for institutional design that will promote human happiness.

Chapter 7 returns to Marcuse's preconditions for the achievement of human happiness in asserting that an order of abundance will require the recognition of a right to livelihood. A right to the social goods necessary to the pursuit of happiness differs from the largely negative rights of liberalism in that it is held, not against any individual or social group, but against society as a whole. It is held against society because it is not the product of individual choice, but the result of a social discovery of our common identity. Indeed, it is only because we share a common identity that we can have positive, unchosen duties to others.

As changes in our basic institutions promote social justice, a new sensibility may emerge which will promote life over death, knowledge over ignorance, pleasure over pain, creation over destruction. With the development of this sensibility, lies the possibility of a genuine happiness.

Chapter 1

The Divided Self

In the American Declaration of Independence, Thomas Jefferson identified the right to life, liberty and the pursuit of happiness as the goals of justice. While our democratic tradition has focused on the right to life and liberty, it has largely ignored the pursuit of happiness.

The reason for this failure is unclear. It may be that the pursuit of happiness is equated with the exercise of liberty. If the two values are synonymous, then the right to liberty and the pursuit of happiness are redundant and the latter need not be considered as a fundamental right.

If, on the other hand, liberty is a necessary, but not a sufficient, condition for the achievement of happiness, the inquiry is more complex. If, in addition to individual liberty, happiness requires social equality, it would be a mistake to equate the pursuit of happiness with the right to liberty. In treating liberty as a sufficient, rather than only as a necessary condition, the importance of both equality and happiness has been undervalued.

If the pursuit of happiness is to be restored as a fundamental right, we must understand its nature. Is the experience of happiness common to all persons? Are there necessary preconditions for the achievement of a general happiness? Should governments limit the liberty of some to promote the happiness of others?

These and other questions about the nature of happiness are the subject of disagreement. Debates about the justice of various institutional arrangements reflect these disagreements. It is my opinion that only by understanding the nature of happiness can we properly evaluate the justice of our social institutions.

When Plato wrote that the just man is happy, and the unjust man miserable, he endorsed the adage that justice is its own reward. For the philosopher John Rawls, justice is the first virtue of social institutions. But for Rawls, and for modern society in general, the connection between justice and happiness is unclear.

In this chapter I discuss the nature of happiness and the preconditions for its achievement. This discussion follows a similar inquiry made by the philosopher Herbert Marcuse, who believed that human happiness requires material abundance, self-knowledge and social justice.

In evaluating Marcuse's claim, we must distinguish happiness from mere satisfaction. Unlike satisfaction, happiness requires knowledge because a person cannot be truly happy unless he both understands the nature of his happiness and has reason to believe that it will persist. A momentary satisfaction is not the same as happiness because, as the proponents of hedonism have noted, many short-term pleasures give rise to long-term pains.

This observation suggests an important connection between time and happiness. Plato maintained that happiness is found in the possession of the good. He also believed that one who possesses good things will want to keep them forever. According to Plato, the desire for the eternal possession of the good reveals a desire for immortality. Because of our mortality, this desire can be achieved only through the generation of offspring or the production of great works.

Plato's discussion of immortality casts a large shadow on the subject of happiness. If immortality is our ultimate desire, then the inevitability of death would seem to preclude the possibility of happiness. On the other hand, the allure of immortality may signify a fundamental truth about our existence. We may desire immortality because the self, unlike the body, is immortal. If so, then the search for self-identity is inseparable from the pursuit of happiness.

In the Western tradition, the philosophic pursuit of happiness began in ancient Greece. For Plato and Aristotle, happiness requires morality. According to their doctrine of eudaemonism, the happy life is the product of virtue, or action in accordance with reason. Because human nature is rational, a common nature yields a common source of happiness. While Plato claimed that virtue is a sufficient condition for happiness,[1] Aristotle insisted on the need for external goods and good fortune in addition to virtue.[2]

In opposition to the eudaemonism of Plato and Aristotle were the proponents of hedonism. In his essay, "On Hedonism," Marcuse contrasted two versions of the hedonistic philosophy—the Cyrenaic and the Epicurean. Within the Cyrenaic school, the pursuit of happiness is secondary to the pursuit of particular pleasures.[3] In addition, the Cyrenaics held that "bodily pleasures are far better than mental pleasures, and bodily pains are far worse than mental pains."[4] The only measure of happiness is the individual's immediate perception of pleasure or pain.

In contrast to the Cyrenaics, the Epicureans adopted what Marcuse labeled a "negative" hedonism. They were not so much interested in obtaining pleasure as they were in avoiding pain. For that reason, he wrote that they "do not choose every pleasure whatsoever, but ofttimes pass over many pleasures when a greater annoyance ensues from them."[5]

Marcuse argued that both schools of hedonism developed in response to the prevailing unhappiness produced by the slave economy in the ancient world. Unfortunately, the hedonists focused their attention solely on the individual and argued that the civic life was something to avoid. Marcuse found fault with hedonism precisely on this point, noting that "[t]he particular interest of the individual, just as it is, is affirmed as the true interest and is justified against every and all community. This is the limit of hedonism: its attachment to the individualism of competition."[6]

According to Marcuse, the failure of hedonism did not lie in its demand for happiness in the face of social injustice, but in its inability to identify the basis for a general happiness. Any theory which endorses the pursuit of pleasure or the avoidance of pain as the only good will be unable to reconcile the interests of individuals with the good of society. Plato anticipated this critique of hedonism when he contended that the gratification of "bad" pleasures could undermine the social order.

In Plato's view, happiness requires knowledge. One must know the good in order to do it. Thus, the pursuit of happiness cannot be divorced from the quest for understanding. This quest has since characterized the theoretical attitude of all science and philosophy.

In his quest to understand the changing and contingent character of reality, Plato developed his theory of forms. In his view, every object of experience is but an imperfect copy of an eternal form. In various dialogues, he discussed the relationship between the form of the good and the possibility of human happiness.

In *The Republic*, for example, Plato used the analogy of the cave in order to distinguish the form of the good as the ultimate truth from our false notions of the material world.[7] In the analogy, he contrasted the vision of prisoners who can only view shadows cast on the wall by figures passing outside of their cave with that of the person who emerges from the cave to see the real world bathed in sunlight. Plato held that the person who emerges from the darkness of false notions into the light of reason must return to the cave to free those who are still imprisoned there. In making this claim, he explained that the purpose of philosophical education is not to bring about the happiness of a particular individual or class of individuals, but of the entire population.

Plato continued his discussion of happiness in the *Symposium,* where he described a banquet at which a number of orators are asked to explain the nature of love. Aristophanes told a story of how humans are divided in two at birth and that our pursuit of romantic love represents the attempt to be reunited with our severed half. He used this story to explain homosexuality. Thus, if our other half was of the same sex we would be naturally attracted to members of our own sex. This tale of physical division was incorporated into Socrates's final speech in which he explained that we are always striving after what we lack.

In this speech, Socrates described the instruction he received from the wise woman, Diotima of Mantineia. Diotima informed Socrates that love is neither mortal nor immortal, good nor bad, beautiful nor ugly. Born of poverty and plenty, love is always striving after what it lacks. However, we do not love the ugly or the bad because only possession of beauty and good things brings happiness. Because one who possesses perfect beauty or goodness would want to keep it forever, the ultimate object of love is immortality. For finite creatures, a measure of immortality may be attained through the "birth in beauty" of natural offspring as well as the products of the soul.

In the dialogue, Diotima told Socrates that in order to grasp the essence of beauty:

> he should love one body and there beget beautiful speech; then he should take notice that the beauty in one body is akin to the beauty in another....When he has learnt this, he must become the lover of all beautiful bodies.... Next he must believe beauty in souls to be more precious than beauty in the body...that he may moreover be compelled to contemplate the beauty in our pursuits and customs, and to see that all beauty is of one and the same kin.... Next he must be led from practice to knowledge. . .directing his gaze from now on towards beauty as a whole . . . and in contemplation of it give birth to many beautiful and magnificent speeches and thoughts in the abundance of philosophy.[8]

Diotima further stated that the nature of beauty is everlasting, neither increasing nor diminishing. While beautiful things are born and perish, beauty remains unchanged. As such, it is both perfect and immortal. For Plato, beauty, as the form of the good, represents our highest aspiration—the promise of happiness.

Plato's observations in the *Symposium* deserve careful scrutiny. In the dialogue, he wrote that we are constantly striving for what we lack. The ignorant seek knowledge, the poor seek wealth, the sick seek health, and so on. If the self has been divided, we may be said to be seeking unity.

Plato also held that we are drawn to immortality and to the form of the good. We seek the good because only goodness brings happiness. We seek immortality because one who is happy will wish to remain in this state forever. Nietzsche echoed Plato's sentiment when he proclaimed that all joy loves eternity.

However, because human beings are mortal, we can achieve a measure of immortality through the birth in beauty of natural offspring or the products of the soul. Plato had philosophy in mind here, and our reception of his works has provided him with a measure of immortality.

These observations from the *Symposium* address many of the same issues identified by Marcuse in his exploration of human happiness. In his rejection of hedonism, Plato anticipated Marcuse's critique of possessive individualism. Plato's emphasis on immortality foreshadowed Marcuse's conclusion that the reality of death presents a final obstacle to the attainment of happiness. Finally, his examination of eternal beauty as the source of human happiness is consistent with Marcuse's turn to the aesthetic dimension as the determinate negation of class society.

Despite these parallels, Marcuse was critical of the ancient preoccupation with reason as our essential nature. The origin of Plato's philosophy of reason can be seen in the *Phaedrus,* where he described a divided self in the form of a charioteer and his steeds. Reason (the charioteer) must use one horse (spirit) to control the movement of the other (desire) in order to avoid disaster.[9] Because Plato equated the form of the good exclusively with the exercise of reason, he regarded the pursuit of physical pleasure as something to be avoided.

There is little doubt that the philosophy of reason has contributed to the development of repressive morality and hierarchical social organization. While Plato and Aristotle may have been correct to claim that happiness requires virtue, Greek society was constructed on a slave system that made a general happiness impossible.

In "The Concept of Essence," Marcuse acknowledged this contradiction in the philosophy of reason when he noted that the ancients understood human nature as potentiality in conflict with existence. According to Marcuse: "The Being of things is not exhausted in what they immediately are; they do not appear as they could be."[10] In sum, the human capacity to reason did not find expression in a rational social order.

The conflict between essence and appearance has played a critical role in the development of Western philosophy and the pursuit of human happiness. According to Marcuse, idealist philosophers have refused to equate the truth of being with mere appearance. Likewise, in his own critical theory of society, Marcuse held that the truth is not defined by the facts of social existence, but by the unrealized possibilities.

Marcuse did concur with the ancient dictum that happiness requires knowledge when he wrote that: "Happiness is not in the mere feeling of satisfaction but in the reality of freedom and satisfaction. Happiness involves knowledge: it is the prerogative of the animal rationale."[11] As we will see, the necessity of self-knowledge will play a central role in any inquiry into the possibility of human happiness.

Marcuse also maintained that the interest in social justice produced a tension within classical theory which could not be resolved within the context of the slave economy. However, despite this unresolved tension, classical theory reflected an accommodation to the social order in three ways. First, Aristotle's delineation of active and passive reason, with the latter reserved for the slave, reflected the prevailing order of domination and servitude. Second, the separation of practical from philosophical knowledge reinforced the belief that a general happiness is not to be found in this world. Third, the otherworldly appeal of both the Platonic and Aristotelian world views utilized reason as a means to repress the erotic and aggressive instincts at work within the human psyche.

As we have seen, the appeal to reason in classical philosophy coexisted with an irrational social order. The philosophical contemplation of the good did not produce a general happiness. On the contrary, classical philosophy resigned itself to the fact that happiness was not to be found in this world.

This spirit of resignation grew deeper in the feudal period as Christian theologians used reason and religion to create an elaborate idea of the afterlife. But unlike Plato's reconciliation of the tension between essence and existence as idealist critique, Christian theology pacified the tension with the idea of a loving God. This idea reduced social conflict while deferring the promise of happiness to the "other world."

Subsequently, in the bourgeois era, the philosopher Immanuel Kant also defined human nature in terms of our rational capabilities, but his conception of reason rested upon two distinct conceptions. Kant defined reason as both the unifying totality of the cognitive faculty and as "a single faculty that rises 'above' the understanding, as the faculty of those 'Ideas' that can never be represented in experience."[12]

It is only the latter conception of reason, that of a purely regulative function, which possesses any relation to freedom in Kant's philosophy. That freedom, of course, is internal. Freedom is understood as the ability of the subject to give to itself the universally necessary laws of reason. External to the individual is a world governed by natural necessity. Consequently, the critical function of reason is restricted to the realm of morality as the only realm which can be determined in accordance with the rule of freedom.

Marcuse interpreted the appeal to reason in Kant's philosophy as reflective of the nature of bourgeois society. The universal freedom proclaimed by that society masks the reality that the "free" economic subjects are controlled by the laws of the commodity market. The emphasis on duty and morality contained in Kant's philosophy underscores the extent to which happiness is not something one should expect to achieve. In fact, the pursuit of happiness is a subversive idea which finds expression only in bourgeois art.

Marcuse asserted that because "the beauty of art is compatible with the bad present," bourgeois art is able to offer happiness in an illusory form. Bourgeois culture makes eternal the beautiful moment which can be repeated again and again in the art work. He noted that "[t]here is an element of earthly delight in the works of great bourgeois art.... The individual enjoys beauty, goodness, splendor, peace and victorious joy. He even enjoys pain and suffering, cruelty and crime. He experiences liberation."[13] It is, however, only the liberation of the moment. Happiness is possible only in the aesthetic illusion.

In contrast with the views of Plato and Kant, Karl Marx offered a new interpretation of human nature. He argued that the "essence of man is no abstraction inhering in each single individual. In its actuality it is the ensemble of social relationships."[14]

Marx also maintained that we are sensuous beings whose nature is confirmed by the products of our labor as a practical activity. Thus, human beings do not simply receive the objective world, we appropriate it by transforming objects into the organs of our life. For that reason, our essential powers are confirmed only through their objectification.

Marx further argued that objective reality is social and historical. He characterized the nature of social relationships in all class societies as one of domination and servitude. Beginning with the first division of labor, one class of persons has labored for another. For that reason, neither class can realize itself in its labor.[15]

Marx analyzed the problem of alienated labor at length in his *Economic and Philosophic Manuscripts of 1844*. In that work, he argued that in class societies the worker is alienated both from the product of labor and from the labor process itself. Because the object which labor produces belongs not to the worker but to another, it confronts the worker as something alien. Consequently, his productive life appears only as a means to another end.[16]

Furthermore, the alienation of labor leads to other forms of alienation, including the alienation from nature, from other human beings, and from the species being which binds humans into community. For Marx, historical materialism represents a "real humanism" which grasps the alienation of labor as a practical problem. Because Marx defined human nature in terms of our capacity to labor, the alienation of labor presents a major impediment to the goal of human happiness.

The implications of Marx's theory of alienation for the problem of human happiness seem clear. First, Marx understood that the possibility of human happiness relies upon the actual state of social conditions. Since objective reality is social and historical, the present form of objective reality must be superseded before a new form can exist. Therefore, he called for a revolution of the proletariat as the only means by which a general happiness could be achieved.

Further, Marx maintained that communism represents the resolution of the tension between essence and existence which first appeared in classical philosophy. According to Marx, communism would represent "the genuine resolution of the conflict between man and nature and between man and man—the true resolution of the strife between existence and essence, between objectification and self-confirmation, between freedom and necessity, between the individual and the species."[17]

In the initial formulations of his critical theory, Marcuse maintained that the realization of reason in society would mean the disappearance of philo-sophy. He argued that historical materialism reversed the orientation of all pre-vious conceptions of humanity. In Marxism, "the idea of reason has been super-seded by the idea of happiness."[18]

In contrast to traditional philosophy, Marcuse insisted that: "The philosophical construction of reason is replaced by the creation of a rational society."[19] In such a society, individuals could collectively regulate their lives in accordance with their needs.

Writing in the 1930's, Marcuse believed that the real potentialities for the fulfillment of human life were at hand. The relative success of capitalism in overcoming material scarcity had provided the level of economic development which Marx saw as necessary for socialist transformation. Marcuse believed that human fulfillment would be determined by such factors as the control of natural and social productive forces, the development of needs in relation to the possibility of their satisfaction, and the availability and wealth of cultural values.[20]

Above all, Marcuse believed that democratic social planning could enable persons to freely decide what was to be produced and how the wealth of society would be distributed. This emphasis on democracy and the autonomy of assoc- iated individuals characterized his vision of the rational society. The purpose of critical theory, therefore, was to explore the actual tendencies within capital- ist society which could provide the basis for the realization of this society.

Although Marcuse's hope for social revolution was shattered by the defeat of proletarian movements in Europe, he continued to develop his critical theory. Unlike Marx, however, his indictment of social domination focused on the suc- cess of the capitalist system in assimilating its opponents with the promise of an ever-increasing material standard of living. As early as 1941, he argued that the proletariat no longer represented the determinate negation of society and that "the coordinated masses do not crave a new social order but only a larger share in the prevailing one."[21] Consequently, he believed that if the working class is to become radicalized, the catalysts of change must come from outside its ranks.

Following the second World War, Marcuse turned his attention to the works of Sigmund Freud. Freud and the philosopher Friedrich Nietzsche had written about the self in a manner that evoked Marx's analysis of alienated labor, although neither embraced his call for social revolution.

Both Freud and Nietzsche saw inner conflict as a source of unhappiness. Nietzsche described the conflict as one between a "will to power" and a "will to nothing." Following Nietzsche, Freud coined the term "death instinct" to describe the urge to return to the peacefulness of inorganic existence. He further characterized the conflict within the self as one between the id and the superego with the id representing the self's unrestrained pursuit of pleasure and the superego representing the critical judgment of society. According to Freud, this conflict has produced a "dialectic of civilization" which requires ever greater repression of our instinctual desires as society makes cultural and scien-tific progress.[22]

In 1955, Marcuse made one of the first attempts to reconcile the views of Marx and Freud with the publication of *Eros and Civilization*. Despite its pes- simistic implications, Marcuse adopted Freud's instinct theory. In doing so, he recast *Thanatos*, or the death instinct, not as the urge to death, but as the desire for the elimination of pain. Consequently, as pain and misery are reduced, death "would cease to be an instinctual goal."[23]

While Freud viewed the destructive instincts as largely immutable and forever in need of repression, Marcuse maintained that objective changes in social organization could reduce the aggressive tendencies within the psyche and allow for a much greater measure of freedom and happiness. In *Eros and Civilization*, he utilized his critical theory to demonstrate the objective possibilities for a non-repressive society. He argued for a rational sensuality that could satisfy basic material needs through an equitable system of distribution while also satisfying instinctual needs for peace and pleasure through the development of an aesthetic sensibility.

As it developed in the 1960's, Marcuse's critique of advanced capitalist society was based on three points. First, the permanent preparation for war required the expenditure of huge sums for weapons of destruction which postpone the abolition of scarcity while eliminating any real sense of security. Second, the uneven level of capitalist development has generated a permanent underclass of the dispossessed and unemployable outcasts of society. Third, the needs generated in capitalist society are "false" because their satisfaction represses other "higher" needs. Such higher needs would involve the intellectual and aesthetic aspirations of humanity as well as the realization of solidarity with other human beings.

The issue of false needs played a particularly important role in Marcuse's critical theory because of his belief that Marx's proletariat had dissolved as a revolutionary force. For that reason, he turned his attention to the imagination in order to project a new historical subject for whom revolution might constitute a vital need. This theme was pursued in works such as *An Essay on Liberation* and *Counter-Revolution and Revolt* where Marcuse argued for a new sensibility which would place human happiness before competitive economic pursuits as the goal of social institutions. He believed that the images of freedom and gratification preserved by the imagination could be expressed in works of art. His subsequent turn to the aesthetic dimension represented an attempt to indict existing reality in favor of its repressed, but genuinely human possibilities.

In his final work, *The Aesthetic Dimension*, Marcuse maintained that art "is committed to an emancipation of sensibility, imagination, and reason in all spheres of subjectivity and objectivity."[24] For him, aesthetic form came to replace the proletariat as the determinate negation of existing society. This claim is significant because it represents a theory of revolution which lacks a revolutionary class.

In *The Aesthetic Dimension*, Marcuse also insisted that "no society can transcend what is called chance or fate and that unresolvable contradictions and sorrow are inevitable. One reason for this conclusion is that death denies once and for all the reality of a non-repressive existence."[25] Despite this pessimistic conclusion, Marcuse never abandoned his belief that a new sensibility could reshape our social institutions and bring about a far greater degree of human happiness. His commitment to this project has greatly influenced the present work.

To this point, our examination of the nature of happiness and the divided self reveals a troubling relationship between reason, happiness and social justice. Philosophers since Plato have argued that happiness depends upon the exercise of reason. However, the actual history of Western civilization has shown that the exercise of reason has not brought about a general happiness. In fact, the application of technological rationality has resulted in the development of militarism, industrialization, bureaucracy and globalization—developments which have clearly increased the level of human unhappiness.

The failure of reason to produce a general happiness requires a closer examination of the forces within the human psyche. This examination brings us to Freud and the death instinct.

Chapter 2

The Death Instinct

Freud's metapsychological speculations present a serious challenge to the assumed rationality of the human subject. Of particular interest to Marcuse was Freud's hypothesis of a death instinct present in organic life since its origin.

Nietzsche addressed the existence of a death instinct in *The Birth of Tragedy* when he described it as a will to decline.[1] He also referred to the instinct as a will to nothing in contrast to a will to power which he saw as the animating life force. Nietzsche claimed that under the influence of Christianity, nineteenth century society had developed a herd mentality which repressed the will to power. In response to this manifestation of the death instinct, he proposed a transvaluation of values in which individuals would will the eternal return of the same. He believed that a person who could affirm life just as it is would be free from the spirit of resentment which condemns us to lives of mediocrity and unhappiness.

In *The Birth of Tragedy*, Nietzsche contrasted the Apollinian and Dionysian strands within Greek tragedy. He wrote that Apollo symbolizes the beautiful illusion and the principle of individuation. Dionysus represents intoxication and sexual frenzy, in other words, the collapse of individuation. According to Nietzsche, the Dionysian festival:

> centered in extravagant sexual licentiousness, whose waves overwhelmed all family life and its venerable traditions; the most savage natural instincts were unleashed.... At the very climax of joy there sounds a cry of horror or a yearning lamentation for an irretrievable loss. In these Greek festivals, nature seems to reveal a sentimental trait; it is as if she were heaving a sigh at her dismemberment into individuals.... In the Dionysian dithyramb man is incited to the greatest exaltation of all his symbolic faculties; something never before experienced struggles for utterance—the annihilation of the veil of *maya*, oneness as the soul of the race and of nature itself.[2]

Nietzsche's depiction of the Dionysian state as the annihilation of the veil of *maya* asserts a metaphysical claim advanced by the adherents of Buddhism and Hinduism. For them, *maya* represents illusion. On this view, the world of appearance is illusory, concealing behind it the unity of self and world. To annihilate the veil of *maya* is to understand the real nature of things. Just as Plato held that individuals are copies of eternal forms, for Nietzsche, the Dionysian dithyramb reveals a unity prior to Apollinian individuation.

Freud's metapsychology was inspired both by Nietzsche's claim of an underlying unity of self and world and by his claim of a fundamental struggle between the will to power and the will to nothing. Freud described this struggle as one between the life and the death instincts. He defined an instinct as "an urge inherent in organic life to restore an earlier state of things which the living entity has been obliged to abandon under the pressure of external disturbing forces."[3]

The earlier state of things to which Freud referred is the inorganic state. His clinical observations led him to conclude that: "The dominating tendency of mental life... is the effort to reduce, to keep constant or to remove internal tension due to stimuli... and our recognition of that fact is one of our strongest reasons for believing in the existence of death instincts."[4]

Freud's hypothesis of a death instinct was first proposed in *Beyond the Pleasure Principle*. Patient accounts of the repetition of traumatic dreams and painful behavior patterns led him to posit the existence of an instinct which opposes the pleasure principle. Freud proposed that a death instinct could explain an irrational inclination to pain. The existence of sadomasochism also provided evidence of the fusion of sexual, aggressive and self-destructive instincts.

In addition to a death instinct, Freud also believed that the inclination to aggression represents "an original, self-subsisting instinctual disposition in man [and] it constitutes the greatest impediment to civilization."[5] Because of our innate aggressiveness, Freud believed that civilization is necessarily built upon the repression of the human instinctual constitution.

In *Beyond the Pleasure Principle*, Freud traced the maturation of his instinct theory from its initial division of the ego and sexual instincts. With his hypothesis of narcissistic libido, the sexual instinct was transformed into Eros, "which seeks to force together and hold together the portions of living substance."[6]

Sexuality designated that portion of *Eros* which is directed toward objects. Freud speculated that *Eros* operates from the beginning of life as a "life instinct" in opposition to a "'death instinct' which was brought into being by the coming to life of inorganic substance."[7]

Freud then concluded that his original characterization of the ego instincts as separate from the sexual instincts was challenged by his realization that a portion of the ego instincts had a libidinal quality which took the subject's own ego as its object. He wrote that:"These narcissistic self-preservative instincts had thence-forward to be counted among the libidinal sexual instincts."[8]

The distinction between the ego and sexual instincts was thus transformed into one between ego and object instincts, both of which were of a libidinal nature. Freud explained that at this point a new opposition emerged between the libidinal instincts and the instincts at work in destructive behavior. He referred to this opposition as one between the life instincts and the death instincts, characterized as *Eros* and *Thanatos*.

Although Marcuse adopted Freud's theory of a death instinct, his application of it remains somewhat obscure. In *Eros and Civilization*, he argued that the ultimate goal of the instinct is pleasure rather than death, writing: "If the instinct's basic objective is not the termination of life but of pain—the absence of tension—then paradoxically, in terms of the instinct, the conflict between life and death is the more reduced, the closer life approximates the state of gratification.... Death would cease to be an instinctual goal."[9]

Although Marcuse believed that our instincts are essentially conservative, he rejected Freud's designation of them as immutable. Rather, he argued that the aggressiveness which Freud found to be innate in human beings is nothing more than a depiction of the domination historically present in class societies. Accordingly, he argued that a change in social organization could result in a modification of our instinctual constitution.

Marcuse also appropriated several other features of Freud's metapsychology, including a tripartite division of the self into id, ego and superego. According to Freud, the id is the most archaic structure of the self. It is governed entirely by the pleasure principle, Freud's term for the desire for a diminution of the quantity of excitation.[10]

The ego represents the self-conscious organization of the human personality. The existence of scarcity has led to the emergence of a reality principle which requires the ego to postpone or abandon many of the pleasures sought by the id in the interest of self-preservation.

Finally, the superego incorporates society's demands on the individual. According to Freud, the need to establish and enforce order requires the repression of aggressive tendencies in individuals. This introjection of aggression produces conscience, the sense of guilt and the need for punishment.[11]

The demands of the superego struggle against the urges of the id for control of the ego. Freud noted that in the process of maturation our sense of our self changes significantly. For the infant:

the ego includes everything, later it separates off an external world from itself. Our present ego-feeling is, therefore, only a shrunken residue of a much more inclusive—indeed, an all-embracing—feeling which corresponded to a much more intimate bond between the ego and the world about it.[12]

Freud called this feeling oceanic and referred to the impulse to return to this state as the Nirvana principle. Marcuse speculated that: "Perhaps the taboo on incest was the first great protection against the death instinct: the taboo on Nirvana, on the regressive impulse for peace which stood in the way of progress, of Life itself."[13]

Marcuse also adopted Freud's evolutionary theory. According to this theory, at the genesis of organic life is the realization that life is less satisfactory, or more painful, than the preceding inorganic stage. This awareness generates the death instinct as "the drive for relieving this tension through regression."[14]

The next turning point in Freud's theory occurs at the origin of civilization when the existence of scarcity forces the repressive control of the instincts. Freud speculated that the first human group was dominated by the father on the basis of his physical prowess. In this primal horde, the father monopolized the women while the instinctual energy of his sons was diverted to work. Eventually, their repression culminated in a rebellion in which they collectively killed and devoured the father and established the brother clan.

There was an ambivalence in the brothers' attitude toward their father, however. Their hatred was mixed with admiration and affection because the father provided the order necessary to maintain the group. Their collective guilt felt upon the destruction of this order led them to deify the father and to establish a sexual taboo enforced by the clan as a whole.[15]

Freud's general theory of social evolution was very much informed by the above speculation. He believed that the presence of guilt was central to the development of civilization. Although this speculation is beyond the realm of anthropological verification, Marcuse accepted it for its symbolic value. What is more, he asserted that the alleged consequences of these events are historical facts.

With the publication of *Eros and Civilization* in 1966, Marcuse made a serious attempt to reconcile Freud's metapsychology, especially the death instinct, with Marxism and the western philosophical tradition. Although neither Marx nor the proletariat are mentioned in the first edition of the work, the insights of Marxism are incorporated into its general framework. In attempting to reconcile the theories of Marx and Freud, Marcuse attempted to demonstrate that a non-repressive civilization is theoretically possible.

Marcuse began his introduction to this work with the observation that: "Sigmund Freud's proposition that civilization is based on the permanent subjugation of the human instincts has been taken for granted."[16] While adopting many of Freud's speculations, he sought to overcome the apparent biologism of the Freudian system. Where Freud saw the struggle for existence as an eternal condition of humanity, Marcuse contended that it would be possible to gradually reduce the level of instinctual repression.

In *Eros and Civilization*, Marcuse acknowledged that the presence of scarcity has led to the emergence of a reality principle which represses the instinctual demands of the id. He coined the term "performance principle" to describe the historical form of this reality principle and with this term he argued that individuals are judged in class society by their competitive economic performances.[17] While Marcuse accepted the fact that "scarcity teaches men that they cannot freely gratify their instinctual impulses," he rejected the claim that scarcity depicts an eternal fate of humanity.[18] Although couched in the language of psychoanalysis, his critique of domination was consistent with Marx's historical materialism.

It was Marcuse's contention that at the attained level of mature industrial society, an order of abundance could eliminate the repression and domination enforced by past orders of scarcity. This order of abundance would make possible the emergence of a new sensibility in which instinctual liberation could be harmonized with social order.

That human happiness requires the abolition of scarcity appears uncontroversial. As long as scarcity exists, human needs will go unsatisfied. Indeed, both Marx and Marcuse extolled the technical progress generated by capitalism as the necessary basis for the satisfaction of human needs. However, they also understood that technical progress presented a serious threat to the possibility of a general happiness.

In examining this threat, Marcuse extended his analysis of Freud's metapsychology and the death instinct to technology and what he termed technological rationality. It was not technology *per se*, which he found objectionable, but its utilization as a means of social domination. Like the philosophy of reason, technological rationality represents both a methodology and a world view. Marcuse argued that the domination of nature, which technological rationality encourages, engenders the domination of humankind.

Marcuse's critique of technological rationality focused primarily on the application of scientific rationality to questions of social organization. He defined scientific rationality as that use of reason which, by quantifying nature, separates the true from the good, science from ethics. Universal ideas are refuted *a priori* by scientific rationality. They become "mere ideals, and their concrete content evaporates."[19]

According to Marcuse, scientific rationality pretends to remove the interest of the observing subject from the object of study. But the appropriation of science by the dominant forces in society betrays its professed disinterestedness. Because scientific knowledge always exists within a political context, the application of science to technology necessarily involves either an extension or a subversion of the existing political order.

For Marcuse, the forces that control society have used technology to bolster their domination. He held that when the domination of human beings is accomplished through the use of technology, scientific rationality becomes technological rationality. According to Marcuse, technological rationality represents the constriction of reason to the needs of the technical apparatus. No longer is the satisfaction of human needs the ultimate goal of reason. Rather, the rational is defined in terms of what serves the interest of the apparatus.

Marx had argued that the alienation of the worker from the product of labor led to the fetishism of commodities in which a "definite social relation between men ... assumes the fantastic form of a relation between things."[20] For him, the fetishism of commodities concealed the true nature of capitalism as a system of domination and servitude.

In Marcuse's critical theory, the fetish of technique, or technical efficiency, replaced commodity fetishism as the predominant form of mystification in the modern world.[21] For him, social organization as a whole reflects a technological *a priori* which defines all social relationships in terms of technical efficiency. As a consequence, individuals develop a matter-of-fact attitude which does not question the efficacy of technological rationality.[22]

Marcuse argued that the organization of modern society reflects a machine process which subordinates individual differences to a common framework of standardized performances. The pursuit of profit dictates the quantity, form and kind of commodities that are produced and the skills of the individual laborer tend to be reduced to a series of "semi-spontaneous reactions to prescribed mechanical norms."[23]

This application of technological rationality to social organization finds its clearest expression in bureaucracy. Marcuse cited Weber's dictum that: "'In contrast to the democratic self-administration of small homogeneous units', bureaucracy is 'the universal concomitant of modern mass democracy.'"[24] The development of bureaucratic organization is also the universal concomitant of the technical apparatus.

Bureaucratization embodies the whole of the advanced capitalist and socialist world. It is central to both public and private organizations, to the ruling elite and to the official opposition. Bureaucracies function hierarchically in order to regulate, control, enhance, and maintain the efficient utilization of resources, both human and natural, within a society defined by the economic performances of its members.

Although the bureaucratization of society is hardly synonymous with fascism, Marcuse believed that technological rationality was common to both forms of organization. He argued that fascism represents an extreme form of bureaucratic organization guided by a technological rationality unchecked by any overriding concern for human happiness.[25] By equating reason with the needs of technical efficiency, our rulers can transform the rational self-interest of individuals into compliance with the demands of the state. In this manner, the connection between reason and happiness, the object of philosophy from the beginning of Western civilization, is severed.[26]

Marcuse's Frankfurt School associate, Theodor Adorno, also made use of Freudian theory in his analysis of fascism. Adorno believed that a death instinct could be discerned in the yearning to merge one's ego with that of others in a fascist community. In "Freudian Theory and the Pattern of Fascist Propaganda," Adorno adopted Freud's theory of projection to explain the appeal of fascism.[27] Freud held that in a mass, individual identities merge with the identity of the group as personified by its leader. In the process, the individual is free to throw off the repressions of his unconscious instincts.

According to Adorno: "The formation of the imagery of an omnipotent and unbridled father figure…is the only way to promulgate the 'passive-masochistic attitude…'an attitude required of the fascist follower the more his political behavior becomes irreconcilable with his own rational interests."[28] The resulting "fascist community of the people corresponds exactly to Freud's definition of a group as being 'a number of individuals who have substituted one and the same object for their ego ideal and have consequently identified themselves with one another in their ego.'"[29]

According to Adorno, this group identification allows group members to project their own self-hatred onto the members of outgroups.[30] The concentration of hostility onto outgroups relieves the intolerance one feels for one's own group.

The projection of hostility onto others represented for Nietzsche an expression of the death instinct. He saw the instinct at work in Christianity and in efforts to repress individual expression. If the death instinct represents a judgment that conscious life is unsatisfactory, then its projection would produce aggression and exploitation while its internalization would result in guilt and submission to authority. If this view is correct, then the history of domination and servitude may be attributed to a death instinct inherent in consciousness.

In sum, the critique of technological rationality as a form of mystification and domination goes to the heart of our concern for human happiness. Happiness involves knowledge; it requires the exercise of reason in a world free from fear, want and anxiety. Technological rationality, however, has constricted reason to the end of technical efficiency. That end has displaced the development of other human abilities. Consequently, technology cannot deliver the happiness it promises because human happiness is no longer its goal. As long as reason is applied primarily to questions of technical efficiency, it is powerless to criticize and transcend existing social relationships.[31]

In response to the problem of technological rationality, Marcuse proposed the idea of a new science and technology. He believed that the order of domination promoted by scarcity could be abolished because of the technical progress fostered by a capitalist division of labor. In *An Essay on Liberation*, for example, he argued that what is needed is "not the arrest or reduction of technical progress, but the elimination of those features which perpetuate man's subjection to the apparatus."[32] He also believed that the emergence of new needs which capitalism cannot satisfy would, accordingly, lead to the development of a new science and technology.

As noted above, Marcuse's critique of technological rationality is based on the belief that the order of abundance achieved in the advanced industrial nations has created "transcending needs which cannot be satisfied without abolishing the capitalist mode of production."[33] The satisfaction of these new needs would replace the performance principle with an aesthetic ethos as our new reality principle.

As he developed his critique, Marcuse envisioned a new sensibility which would affirm the "ascent of the life instincts over aggressiveness and guilt" by creating "a vital need for the abolition of injustice and misery."[34] This sensibility would be guided by the imagination and technique would tend toward art. The sensuous, the playful, the calm and the beautiful characterize the aesthetic ethos which he believed would replace the prevailing performance principle.

Moreover, Marcuse's conception of instinctual liberation envisioned our reconciliation with nature. In his search for a new cultural model he turned to Greek mythology and the figures of Narcissus and Orpheus. He observed that: "Theirs is the image of joy and fulfillment...the redemption of pleasure, the halt of time, the absorption of death; silence, sleep, night, paradise."[35]

In these myths the harmony of the human and the natural is restored. "In being spoken to, loved, and cared for, flowers and springs and animals appear as what they are—beautiful, not only for those who address and regard them, but for themselves, objectively."[36]

Marcuse's depiction of our reconciliation with nature challenges the power of the death instinct and the performance principle. His new sensibility promotes the ascent of *Eros* over the aggressive and self-destructive instincts. It envisions human solidarity, environmental harmony, the preservation of joy, and the abolition of alienation, want and privation.

This conception of a new sensibility also calls for a new relationship with nature that would be free from domination. The idea of letting-be characterizes an essentially passive or receptive relationship to the natural world. At the same time, Marcuse acknowledged that receptivity meets the resistance of matter in that "nature is not a manifestation of 'spirit', but rather its essential limit."[37]

This acknowledgment of the limits of receptivity may also be applied to the idea of instinctual liberation. While Marcuse's call for a new science and a new technology might redefine our relationship to nature, it cannot eliminate all ideas of utility. Likewise, even his most optimistic vision of instinctual liberation was restrained by his acceptance of death as the ultimate barrier to lasting gratification.

So while material abundance qualifies as a social precondition for the achievement of happiness, the means by which abundance is attained is problematic. If happiness requires both the abolition of scarcity and the redefinition of our relationship to nature, then a general happiness may be impossible. Even if it is theoretically possible, there will be a continuing tension between our new sensibility and our old calculus of utility. Nature is not only the limit of spirit, it is also the material with which we shape our lives. As such, we must exercise some dominion over the natural world, even if the extent of that dominion may be reduced.

In exploring Marcuse's proposed reconciliation with nature, there is one other fact of existence that must be considered—the inevitability of death. In *Eros and Civilization*, Marcuse concluded that our mortality renders lasting happiness impossible when he wrote that:

> The brute fact of death denies once and for all the reality of a non-repressive existence.... Timelessness is the ideal of pleasure.... But the ego ... is in its entirety subject to time.... The flux of time helps men to forget what was and what can be: it makes them oblivious to the better past and the better future.[38]

Against the surrender to time, Marcuse proposed "the restoration of remembrance to its rights, as a vehicle of liberation."[39] His emphasis on remembrance, however, was not meant to invoke a golden past. Instead, he claimed that it represented an attempt to reassemble the fragments of joy and truth that can be found in a distorted humanity and a distorted nature. For him, the expression of that repressed truth is confined to authentic works of art. It was, therefore, to the aesthetic dimension and the idea of beauty that he returned in his final inquiry into the possibility of human happiness.

In his search for a human faculty free from the repressive control of the performance principle, Marcuse pursued Freud's claim that the imagination is the only human faculty still committed to the pursuit of pleasure. Marcuse noted the decisive function the imagination plays in our total mental structure, when he wrote that: "It links the deepest layers of the unconscious with the highest products of consciousness (art), the dream with the reality; it preserves the archetypes of the genus, the perpetual but repressed ideas of the collective and individual memory, the tabooed images of freedom."[40]

But, despite the critical role which Marcuse assigned to the imagination, he also acknowledged its subservience to the reality principle. According to Marcuse, when the reality principle takes root, "reason prevails: it becomes unpleasant but useful and correct; phantasy remains pleasant but becomes useless, untrue—a mere play, day dreaming."[41]

Nevertheless, the imagination remains essential to any possible reconciliation of reason and happiness. The imagination reinvigorates the tension between existence and essence, between the actual and the possible. According to Marcuse, the cognitive function of the imagination reveals the aesthetic form as the actual expression of the pleasure principle. He asserted that: "Behind the aesthetic form lies the repressed harmony of sensuousness and reason—the eternal protest against the organization of life by the logic of domination, the critique of the performance principle."[42]

The development of Marcuse's aesthetic ethos was influenced considerably by the theories of Kant and Friedrich Schiller. In his *Critique of Judgment*, Kant described aesthetic judgment as the "middle term" between reason and the understanding. He held that contemplation of beautiful objects stimulated the harmonious interplay of the understanding and the imagination. Beauty was designated as "purposiveness without purpose." Just as truth is the object of theoretical reason, and goodness the object of practical reason, beauty is the object of aesthetic judgment. Like truth and goodness, beauty was for Kant a symbolic representation of freedom.[43]

Turning to Schiller, Marcuse observed that: "Only because beauty is a necessary condition of humanity can the aesthetic function play a decisive role in reshaping civilization.... In a truly free civilization, all laws are self-given by the individuals: 'to give freedom by freedom is the universal law' of the aesthetic state."[44]

In contrast to the predominant thought of the bourgeois period, Schiller introduced the concept of the play impulse as an alternative to toil. Its object is beauty, its goal freedom. Marcuse argued that: "[I]n a genuinely humane civilization. the human existence will be play rather than toil, and man will live in display rather than need."[45]

But since time is the fatal enemy of lasting gratification, Schiller attributed to the play impulse the function of "'abolishing time in time', of reconciling being and becoming; change and identity.'"[46] Schiller's call for the timeless possession of beauty echoed the instruction Socrates received from Diotima. All love is ultimately love of immortality.

In *An Essay on Liberation, Counter-Revolution and Revolt* and *The Aesthetic Dimension*, the relationship between beauty and the possibility of happiness is increasingly thematized. Like Plato before him, Marcuse regarded the study of beauty to be essential to the pursuit of self-knowledge. As the embodiment of eternity, the idea of the beautiful counteracts the constriction of reason to the ends of the apparatus. In upholding *Eros* as the goal of social organization, the beautiful becomes an essential element in the effort to achieve a general happiness.

In asserting that radical social change depends upon the emergence of a new aesthetic sensibility, Marcuse argued that: "Radical change in con-sciousness is the beginning, the first step in changing social existence: emergence of the new Subject."[47]

Marcuse's new Subject required a new language and a new mode of perceiving the world. In order to project a sensibility free from all forms of domination, he turned to poetry and surrealism as aesthetic forms which could "dissolve the very structure of perception."[48]

This emphasis on aesthetic form, as opposed to the content of the art work, placed Marcuse outside of the mainstream of Marxist aesthetics. In *The Aesthetic Dimension*, for example, he flatly rejected the claim that the authenticity of a work of art is directly related to its political content.[49] Indeed, his commitment to a new sensibility prevented Marcuse from embracing essential elements of Marxist dogma, such as the dictatorship of the proletariat. Instead, the goal of happiness made the endorsement of any form of authoritarian rule impossible.

For Marcuse, the truth of an art work is measured by its content having become form. Aesthetic form is defined by those qualities which make a work a self-contained whole with a structure and order of its own. Aesthetic form transforms reality into illusion and in so doing affirms its commitment to beauty as the ultimate truth of all art.

The revolutionary character of authentic art is confirmed by the fact that art, by its very commitment to beauty, indicts existing society. The indictment estranges its audience from their everyday lives without offering any simple, practical means of reforming their lives. In Beckett's plays, for example, no hope is offered in a political sense, only the message that our reality must change. Art is able to indict reality precisely because it is unreal. As illusion, art can freely portray the unfreedom of persons.

The commitment of art to aesthetic form, however, weakens the indictment contained in the authentic work. According to Marcuse: "The very commitment of art to form vitiates the negation of unfreedom in art.... The form of the work of art invests the content with qualities of enjoyment."[50] This enjoyment derives from the beautiful illusion which the work presents. The resulting catharsis reduces the sense of estrangement and the need to change reality.

Despite this self-limitation, Marcuse held that the idea of beauty remains subversive of the existing order and offers the most powerful alternative to that order. Art is committed to Eros in its fight against social and instinctual repression. According to Marcuse: "Art represents the ultimate goal of all revolutions: the freedom and happiness of the individual."[51]

The relationship between aesthetic form and revolution remains ambiguous in Marcuse's critical theory. He rejected the identification of aesthetic form with political tendency in favor of autonomous works of art. Because he believed that authentic art is the determinate negation of existing society, he held that authentic works must not uphold any particular social group or political party as the revolutionary vanguard. Instead, Marcuse argued that while art cannot change the world, "it can contribute to changing the consciousness and drives of the men and women who could change the world."[52] At present, these men and women belong to no particular social class, but rather constitute those persons for whom revolution has become a vital need. If social revolution is to take place, it will be necessary to first change the needs of the men and women who could change the world.

The idea that social change requires a change in the structure of our needs epitomizes both the strength and the weakness of Marcuse's critical theory. On one hand, it is clear that class society and technological rationality enforce an order of domination and servitude. On the other, the fact of death prevents the emergence of a new sensibility which might overcome this distortion of human reason. While Marcuse turned to art because it remains committed to the idea of eternity, he acknowledged that even authentic works of art cannot transcend our mortality when he concluded that:

> While art bears witness to the necessity of liberation, it also testifies to its limits. What has been done cannot be undone; what has passed cannot be recaptured.... The institutions of a socialist society, even in their most democratic form, could never resolve all the conflicts between the universal and the particular, between human beings and nature, between individual and individual.[53]

Although Marcuse acknowledged that "tragedy is always and everywhere," he also maintained that:

> this insight, inexorably expressed in art, may well shatter faith in progress but it may also keep alive another image and another goal of praxis, namely the reconstruction of society and nature under the principle of increasing the human potential for happiness. The revolution is for the sake of life, not death.[54]

What this revolution would be like and what type of society it might produce remains to be seen. For Marcuse, the power of reason and memory makes it possible to transcend our present conditions by appropriating our past. Our desire for beauty, displayed in works of art, offers the greatest hope for happiness. In authentic art is contained both the indictment of existing reality and the promise of a better future.

While happiness has been acknowledged to represent an end in itself, the possible means to this end vary radically. The social conditions which Marcuse charted as necessary preconditions for the possibility of happiness—an order of abundance, self-knowledge and social justice—remain the task of political practice. The meaning of these terms, however, remain in dispute.

Marcuse maintained that happiness requires knowledge. However, if the truth of existence is tragic, how can this knowledge produce happiness? In response to this dilemma, Schiller introduced the concept of the play impulse as a means of abolishing time in time. Likewise, Nietzsche's myth of the eternal return sought to break the domination of time over life. The poetic and the mystical conceptions of life have proclaimed the identity of subject and object as the ultimate truth of existence. Authentic art also offers the happiness of the beautiful illusion which can be experienced again and again.

It seems that the question of happiness is inseparable from the question of time. Anxiety over the passage of time robs us of the possibility of happiness. Fear and anxiety emerge in relation to a future which threatens to destroy what we love. Want relates the unsatisfactory present to a possibly better future. Freedom from fear, anxiety and want require not only social justice and an order of abundance, but also the abolition of time in time.

If happiness requires knowledge, then a conception of the self as an unchanging subject of consciousness may provide an answer to the problem of time. If the self is not part of time and space, we may be able to transcend time in a way that frees us from the fear of death. After all, it is not death, but the fear of death, which has caused so much unhappiness. If the self is more than the body, then the inevitability of death need not robs us of happiness.

While Marcuse concluded that a lasting happiness is impossible because of the fact of death, his commitment to historical materialism may have colored his conception of the self. If the self is more than its social and material form, it may be possible to transcend the finality of death.

Plato believed that self-knowledge was sufficient for happiness. That is why he claimed that to know the good is to do it. But, as Aristotle noted, ad-ditional goods are needed for a general happiness. Moreover, as social beings, we have needs that require the establishment of a just society.

The demands of social justice have been long debated within our political tradition. Marcuse's commitment to a new sensibility and instinctual liberation represents one vision of the human good to be promoted by the just society. Other political theorists have offered competing conceptions.

In order to better grasp the importance of social justice to human happiness, this study will turn to two competing traditions within the history of political philosophy. These traditions differ both on the nature of the human good and on the role of the state in promoting that good.

Ultimately, these differences will be attributed to different assumptions about the identity of the self. Given these differences, one will necessarily make different judgments about the nature of justice and the best means to achieve human happiness.

Chapter 3

The Right and the Good

As we saw in chapter one, in the ancient world the goal of human happiness was inextricably linked to a particular conception of human nature and the human good. In contrast with the good of the ancients, the priority of the right over the good stands at the center of modern theories of justice. According to John Rawls, the priority of the right marks the dividing line between the ancient and the modern world views.[1] The priority of the right rests upon the twin conceptions of the separateness of persons and the right of individuals to pursue their own conception of the good. The modern view also rejects the idea of virtue as our common good and the role of the state in promoting this good.

The distinction between the teleology of the ancients and the deontology of the moderns may be further clarified as follows. The ancient tradition, also known as perfectionism, upholds an objective conception of the good as action in accordance with virtue. Although human beings are naturally inclined to pursue this good as the source of happiness, we may be mistaken as to its nature. As a society, we have a duty to promote the good of others and to shape institutions and social practices to conform to it. Because human beings are not equally capable of rational deliberation, the state must play an active role in the moral education of its citizens.

The modern tradition, on the other hand, rejects both the claim of a natural inequality between persons and the idea of an objective human good. It takes individual liberty to be essential to human happiness and insists upon the equal right of all persons to pursue their own conceptions of the good within constraints imposed by principles of justice. Consequently, the state must protect the liberty of citizens while remaining neutral with regard to competing conceptions of the good life. While individuals have a duty to respect the rights of others, there is no duty to promote their good.

The modern tradition came into prominence with the liberal revolutions of the eighteenth century. In this tradition, social justice is defined not in terms of virtue or community, but in terms of liberty and equality. The chief task for political theorists has been to reconcile these competing goals.

These traditions also differ in their moral theories. A deontological theory, such as Kant's moral theory, emphasizes our duty to others as separate moral agents. Kant's categorical imperative instructs us to act in such a way that the maxim, or motivation, of our action may serve as a universal law for all rational beings. A deontological theory, therefore, requires that we give everyone their due, both with regard to distributive and retributive justice.

A teleological theory, such as Aristotle's perfectionism or Mill's utilititarianism, seeks to promote a particular end, such as virtue or happiness. For Aristotle, it was the responsibility of the state to promote the moral character of its citizens in order to maintain a harmonious social order. Mill, on the other hand, believed that it was an individual ethical responsibility to promote the greatest good for the greatest number and that individual liberty is an essential aspect of the good life.

In sum, an action is morally correct on deontological grounds only if it respects the rights of others while an action is morally correct on teleological grounds if it promotes the common good. This theoretical conflict has significant implications for the political theory and practice of modern constitutional democracies.

The evolution of social thought from the teleology of the ancients to the deontology of the moderns is also reflected in the development of utilitarianism. Classical utilitarianism shares the perfectionist view that social institutions should promote an objective human good. Unlike the ancients, however, utilitarians reject the claim of a natural inequality. Thus, Jeremy Bentham could state that in the utilitarian calculus everyone is to count for one, and no one for more than one.

However, as agreement on an objective good became increasingly improbable, classical utilitarianism evolved into preference utilitarianism. Rejecting any conception of an objective good, preference utilitarianism holds that social institutions should be arranged in order to maximize the satisfaction of the rational preferences of the greatest number of persons in society. Because preference utilitarianism accords equal consideration to all persons, it cannot rule out any rational preference as unworthy of consideration.

In contrast to preference utilitarianism, deontological liberalism does rule out some preferences as unworthy of consideration. According to Rawls, deontology differs from teleology in that it makes the right prior to the good.[2] By this, he meant that deontological theories of justice impose restrictions on permissible conceptions of the good life by ruling out preferences which infringe upon the rights of others. These restrictions are justified by what Mill termed the "harm principle." According to this principle, individual liberty may be curtailed only to prevent harm to others.

The teleology of the ancients was best expressed by Aristotle who believed that not only are we inclined to pursue the good, we have a duty to do so. Although he disagreed with Plato about the form of the good, he shared the conviction that the state has a moral responsibility to promote the virtue of its citizens. In support of this perfectionist doctrine, he claimed that:

> the happiness of the individual is the same as that of the state.... [I]t is evident that the form of government is best in which every man, whoever he is, can act best and live happily.... If we are right in our view, and happiness is assumed to be acting well, the active life will be the best, both for every city collectively, and for individuals.... Hence it is evident that the same life is best for each individual, and for states and for mankind collectively.[3]

Aristotle's emphasis on the same life of virtue for each individual stands in sharp contrast with the modern view that individuals, within limits, should be free to design their own plans of life. Of course, by "same life" he meant that all persons should live in accordance with the dictates of reason and virtue.

The importance of reason in the ancient world was underscored by Plato's tripartite division of the self. In *The Republic*, he applied the psychological division between the rational, emotional and appetitive aspects of the self to the social order with the myth of the metals. According to this myth, or "noble lie" as Plato characterized it, some persons are born with gold in their veins, some with silver and others with iron and brass. Plato wrote that:

> 'So you are all brothers in the city,' we shall tell them in our fable, 'but while God molded you, he mingled gold in the generation of some, and those are the ones fit to rule, who are therefore the most precious; he mingled silver into the assistants; and iron and brass in farmers and other craftsmen.'[4]

Depending upon one's nature, the citizen is suited for the life of ruler, soldier, farmer or craftsman. Although the myth distorts the truth about human beings, Plato justified its use by the need to develop a social order in which citizens willingly accept their assigned roles.

Aristotle went much further with his belief in the natural inequality of persons when he wrote that: "The actions of a ruler cannot really be honourable, unless he is as much superior to other men as a man is to a woman, or a father to his children, or a master to his slaves."[5] That such sentiments are clearly odious signifies the degree to which the modern tradition has rejected the ancient idea of inequality.

The ancient view of the state as moral authority also contrasts sharply with the modern conception put forth by John Stuart Mill. For Mill, the priority of the right presupposes that the individual is the best judge of his own happiness. In this regard, he wrote that:

> The only freedom which deserves the name is that of pursuing our own good in our own way, so long as we do not attempt to deprive others of theirs or impede their efforts to obtain it.... The ancient commonwealths thought themselves entitled to practice, and the ancient philosophers countenanced, the regulation of every part of private conduct by public authority, on the ground that the State had a deep interest in the whole bodily and mental discipline of every one of its citizens.[6]

For Mill, the battle for religious liberty was the chief impetus for the assertion of individual rights.[7] In defense of these rights, he proposed the harm principle. This principle asserts that "the sole end for which mankind are warranted, individually or collectively, in interfering with liberty of action of any of their number is self-protection.... [T]he only purpose for which power can be rightfully be exercised ... is to prevent harm to others."[8]

According to Mill, the liberty permitted by the harm principle is essential for human happiness. In his view, liberty is necessary both for self-development and for experiments in living.[9] Because happiness also requires knowledge, freedom of thought and conscience are regarded as essential for its realization. Since individuals can best decide for themselves what will lead to their own happiness, where individual action does not produce harm to others the state has no right to restrict individual liberty. For Mill, the priority of the right, far from abandoning the goal of happiness, is central to its realization.

As noted above, the move from the ancient to the modern world view is marked by two significant changes. One, the modern view discounts the ancient belief in virtue as our common good. Two, the modern view affirms the equality of persons in denying to the state the power to promote any particular conception of the good life.

The rejection of the idea of virtue as our common good was advanced by Thomas Hobbes, a seventeenth century English philosopher. Hobbes also speculated on life in a "state of nature" in order to criticize the ancient belief that human beings are by nature social.[10] Because Hobbes conceived the self to be nothing more than matter in motion, and the state to be but an artificial man, he did not see how social order could be preserved without the intervention of an all-powerful sovereign. Because life in a state of nature would be a war of each against all, Hobbes argued that individuals should surrender their natural liberty in return for the security offered by the sovereign. To this end, he wrote that individuals must:

> confer all their power and strength upon one man, or upon one assembly of men, that may reduce all their wills, by plurality of voices, into one will...and therein to submit their wills, every one to his will, and their judgments to his judgment. This is more than consent, or concord; it is a real unity of them all, in one and the same person, made by covenant of every man with every man.[11]

While Hobbes's psychological theory will not be explored here, it is important to note that our psychological traits have developed within society, not within a state of nature. Hobbes made use of a hypothetical state of nature to describe what life would be like without the strictures of government. His belief that human beings are, by nature, selfish and aggressive remains a part of our folk psychology and may explain the appeal of authoritarianism. However, it is unsuitable as a model for a liberal democratic state. The value we accord to individual liberty presupposes that human beings are capable of social cooperation.

In contrast to Hobbes, John Locke believed that the recognition of common interests made unnecessary the complete centralization of political authority. While Locke agreed with Hobbes that persons are equal in a state of nature, he claimed that this equality means that each person has an unqualified right to his own body and to the product of his labor. He argued that it is not possible for individuals to transfer absolute power to the sovereign because "no body can transfer to another more power than he has in himself; and no body has an absolute arbitrary power over himself, or over any other, to destroy his own life, or take away the life or property of another."[12]

While Hobbes described human beings as thoroughly self-interested, the Lockean self is partly altruistic and partly egoistic. While we understand the need to keep our promises and to respect the rights of others, there is a role for a limited sovereign because human imperfection makes some violations of rights inevitable.[13]

According to Locke, individuals form society "for the general preservation of their lives, liberties, and estates, which I call by the general name— property." [14] By property, Locke meant the interest we have in our persons as well as in other goods.[15]

The importance of liberty and property was directly derived from Locke's concern for human happiness as our greatest good. He justified limitations on the exercise of individual liberty in order to promote happiness when he wrote that:

> As therefore the highest perfection of intellectual nature lies in a careful and constant pursuit of true and solid happiness, so the care of ourselves, that we mistake not imaginary for real happiness, is the necessary foundation for our liberty. The stronger ties we have to an unalterable pursuit of happiness in general... as our greatest good, obliged to suspend the satisfaction of our desire in particular cases. Accordingly, the pursuit of happiness served as the foundation of our liberty and justifies limitations of liberty in particular cases.[16]

While Locke believed that human beings have formed societies in order to better secure their happiness, he rejected the idea that the state should enforce a particular conception of the good. Rather, he viewed the state as the product of agreement in which legitimacy is derived from the consent of the governed. He held that: "The only way whereby any one divests himself of his natural liberty, and puts on the bonds of civil society, is by agreeing with other men to join and unite into a community."[17]

The hypothetical state of nature employed by both Hobbes and Locke underscores the extent to which the modern tradition views our social practices to be the product of choice. While the appeal to a state of nature requires governments to justify their rule, it also implies that individuals choose to join society to pursue their private ends.

Locke's democratic theory, however, did more than repudiate the ancient affirmation of social inequality. It marked a significant shift in our conception of human happiness. No longer was it assumed that political or religious elites have any special insight into the human condition. The liberal revolutions of the seventeenth and eighteenth centuries proclaimed the right individuals to be the sole judge of their own happiness.

One of the first rights secured by the liberal state was the right to contract. By creating markets in labor and enclosing the common lands, the liberal state replaced a feudal order marked by hierarchy and clearly defined social roles. In undermining this order, the liberal state also weakened the power of the church to sanction social inequality. In the process, it advanced the right of religious freedom. The right to contract and the separation of church and state remain bedrock principles of our constitutional order.

Offering a somewhat different view of the basis for political legitimacy was the eighteenth century French philosopher Jean-Jacques Rousseau. Working within the ancient tradition, Rousseau rejected both the nascent individualism of political liberalism and the idea of natural inequality espoused by Plato and Aristotle.

Rousseau described the task of political theory in the following manner: "Find a form of association which defends and protects with all common forces the person and goods of each associate, and by means of which each one, while uniting with all, nevertheless obeys only himself and remains as free as before?"[18] He proposed to solve this problem with a modified version of the social contract that provided for the liberty and equality of citizens by requiring each to submit to the general will. In submitting to this will:

> each person gives himself to no one. And since there is no associate over whom he does not acquire the same right that he would grant others over himself, he gains the equivalent of everything he loses, along with a greater amount of force to preserve what he has.

> Each of us places his person and all his power in common under the supreme direction of the general will; and as one we receive each member as an indivisible part of the whole.[19]

Rousseau agreed with Locke that the greatest good consists of liberty and equality. He also believed that it is the responsibility of citizens, acting in concert, to promote this good. But by liberty, Rousseau meant "obedience to the law one has prescribed for oneself."[20] With respect to equality, he noted that:

> we need not mean… that degrees of power and wealth are to be absolutely the same, but rather that, with regard to power, it should transcend all violence and never be exercised except by virtue of rank and laws; and, with regard to wealth, no citizen should be so rich as to be capable of buying another citizen, and not so poor that he is forced to sell himself.[21]

Rousseau's positive conception of liberty as "freedom for" may be distinguished from a negative conception of liberty as "freedom from" affirmed by liberal political theory..[22] His conception of liberty as the freedom to prescribe the law is consistent with the ancient conception of the good. Unlike the ancients, however, this freedom is not granted to a particular class of rulers, but is shared equally by all members of society.

Rousseau's positive conception of liberty anticipated the views of Marx, who criticized capitalism precisely because it forces individuals to sell themselves to secure their livelihood. Moreover, Rousseau's theory of a general will offered a conception of the self similar to Marx's conception of the self as a species being.

Whether one invokes the views of Mill, Locke or Rousseau, it is clear that our liberal political tradition has emphasized the rights of the individual against those of an entrenched ruling elite. While critics may attack liberalism's "universal rights of man" as nothing more than the rights of a new ruling class, the appeal of the idea that political legitimacy requires the consent of the governed is undeniable. On this view, the legitimacy of any government is measured by the happiness of the many, rather than that of the few.

Of course, it remains to be seen how far liberalism has advanced human happiness. One problem for liberal political theory has been its abandonment of the ancient idea of the good. The lack of any consensus on a common good has clearly undermined our sense of community and weakened our democratic institutions. I will argue that this failure can be traced to an inadequate conception of the self and a resulting inability to offer a compelling argument for social equality. While liberal political theory does not invoke a Hobbesian conception of the self as matter in motion, in giving liberty priority over equality, liberal societies have permitted significant disparities of wealth and power which undermine the possibility of happiness.

As noted above, deontological theories of justice are characterized by the priority of the right over the good. This priority has been formulated in various ways. The liberal legal theorist Ronald Dworkin, for example, has argued that the right to equal concern and respect is fundamental while John Rawls has opted for the greatest equal liberty and the difference principle.[23] The latter would require an equal distribution of social goods unless an unequal distribution would benefit the least advantaged.

The libertarian theorist Robert Nozick, on the other hand, has insisted on the right to justly acquire, retain or transfer holdings.[24] Such a right conflicts with Rawls's claim that all persons have a right to a fair share of the primary goods of society. In fact, on Nozick's account, no state-sponsored redistributive effort is justified. When claims of right conflict in this way, each claim must appeal to some metatheoretical principle, grounded in a conception of the human good. All conceptions of the good will rely, in turn, on a theory of self-identity.

The clearest statement of the priority of the right over the good is found in John Rawls's *A Theory of Justice*. According to Rawls, the doctrine of utilitarianism affirms the priority of the good. Rawls labeled utilitarianism a teleological theory because it defines the good independently from the right and then defines the right as that which maximizes the good.[25]

There is, however, a difference between classical utilitarianism and the teleology of the ancients. In opposition to the natural inequality of the ancients, utilitarians have adopted a principle of equality in which, as Bentham noted, everyone is to count for one, and no one for more than one. Henry Sidgwick expressed the equality principle in this way: "The good of any one individual is of no more importance, from the point of view (if I may say so) of the Universe, than the good of any other."[26]

Classical utilitarianism does share with the ancients the belief in an objective human good.[27] In promoting this good, it seeks to obtain the greatest happiness for the greatest number. In contrast, preference utilitarianism is modern in orientation. It differs from the perfectionism of the ancients not only in its commitment to the equality of persons, but also in its definition of the good as the satisfaction of rational desire. In its effort to maximize overall utility, preference utilitarianism affords equal consideration to all rational desires. This position is in accord with the modern idea that individuals should be the sole judge of their own happiness.

Although utilitarianism respects the principle of equality, it has been criticized for its failure to take seriously the separateness of persons. According to Rawls, utilitarianism violates the intuitive notion that individuals have an inviolability "which even the welfare of everyone else cannot override."[28]

Rawls objected to utilitarianism because it generalizes from what is rational for one person to what is rational for many persons, without taking into consideration that intra-life trade-offs fail to take seriously the separateness of persons. In other words, a policy that is socially beneficial and, for that reason, right on utilitarian grounds, may demand the most extreme sacrifices on the part of particular individuals. For Rawls, such demands fail to accord to those persons the equal consideration to which they are entitled.

In *A Theory of Justice*, Rawls proposed a deontological alternative to utilitarian accounts of justice. He adopted Sidgwick's formulation as the classic statement of utilitarianism: "The main idea is that society is rightly ordered, and therefore just, when its major institutions are arranged so as to achieve the greatest net balance of satisfaction summed over all the individuals belonging to it."[29] In response to Sidgwick, Rawls wrote that:

> The striking feature of the utilitarian view of justice is that it does not matter, except indirectly, how this sum of satisfactions is distributed among individuals.... Thus there is no reason in principle why the greater gains of some should not compensate for the lesser losses of others or, more importantly, why the violation of the liberty of a few might not be made right by the greater good shared by the many.... The most natural way, then, of arriving at utilitarianism ... is to adopt for society as a whole the principle of rational choice for one man.... Utilitarianism does not take seriously the distinction between persons.[30]

Rawls found it tempting to suppose that things could be arranged so as to lead to the most good. However, utilitarianism, so conceived, presents serious problems. While it is prudent for a person to forego one satisfaction if to do so will increase his overall satisfaction, when the process is applied to society as a whole, unacceptable results follow. A trade-off between present and future satisfactions is acceptable within a life, but is unacceptable between lives. One person's sacrifice *is* not vindicated because *someone else* has received a greater benefit than would have been possible without the sacrifice. It is this failure to take seriously the distinct claims of persons which renders teleological theories inadequate on Rawls's view.

While Rawls was critical of teleological theories for making the good prior to the right, he developed a theory of justice based on social primary goods such as income and wealth, liberty and opportunity, and the social bases of self-respect which he believed would be adopted by rational contractors. In a famous thought experiment, Rawls described the deliberation of hypothetical contractors meeting behind a "veil of ignorance" in what he called the "original position."

In this position, the mutually disinterested contractors do not know their social position. Under such conditions, Rawls maintained that the contractors would endorse principles insuring the greatest equal liberty and an equal distribution of the social primary goods unless an unequal distribution would benefit the least advantaged. He claimed that contractors would endorse the first principle because it provides them with the liberty necessary to pursue their own conceptions of the good. They would support the second because under conditions of uncertainty it is rational to maximize the minimum position in society.

The theoretical adequacy of justice as fairness would seem to depend both on the goods Rawls takes to be primary and on the assumptions of mutual disinterest and rationality under conditions of uncertainty. Should any of his assumptions prove erroneous, his theory would be undermined. Even if Rawls's assumptions are valid, his theory of justice would not represent the priority of the right over the good in the strictest sense because his principles of justice are based on a "thin theory of the good."

This theory of justice as fairness differs from preference utilitarianism in that it rules out the satisfaction of some rational desires as inconsistent with justice. Rawls wrote that: "The principles of right, and so of justice, put limits on which satisfactions have value; they impose restrictions on what are reasonable conceptions of one's good."[31] In other words, justice as fairness grants us the right to pursue our own conception of the good only if our conception conforms to the principles of justice.

Because there are many different life plans, Rawls believed that indi-viduals will differ in their conceptions of the good. What is good for a person is what allows him to successfully pursue his plan of life. However, Rawls did not believe that rational contractors in the original position would differ in their conceptions of the social primary goods. Because justice as fairness relies upon a theory of the good, it is important to distinguish between the good of an individual and the social primary goods which Rawls held to be common to all.

Rawls referenced the good of the individual when he addressed the value of a plurality of conceptions of the good. Underlying this plurality, however, is a conception of the common good. Indeed, Rawls wrote that when Hume criticized Locke's contract theory on behalf of utility, "[u]tility [for Hume] seems to be some form of the common good.... If this interpretation of Hume is correct, there is offhand no conflict with the priority of justice."[32]

Rawls went on to point out that: "Government is assumed to aim at the common good, that is, at maintaining conditions and achieving objectives that are similarly to everyone's advantage."[33] He described the common good "as certain general conditions that are in an appropriate sense equally to everyone's advantage."[34]

That justice as fairness aims at a common good can also be seen in the concept of political legitimacy. If government in the modern tradition is based on the consent of the governed, then principles of justice in a liberal democracy must advance the common good if they are to create political obligation.

If Rawls's principles of justice, adopted on the basis of a hypothetical social consensus, uphold a conception of the common good, then justice as fairness does not represent as radical a departure from the teleology of the ancients as Rawls believed. Seen in this light, justice as fairness is not premised on the priority of the right over the good; rather it defines the right as that which maximizes the common good.[35] While this definition of the right distinguishes justice as fairness from utilitarianism, it shares with the perfectionism of the ancients the belief that not all desires are worthy of consideration. It differs from perfectionism in what it takes to constitute our common good. For justice as fairness, liberty and equality, not virtue or human excellence, define our good.

If deontological theories of justice invoke a conception of a common good, then the real debate over the nature of justice does not concern the priority of the right or the good, but the nature of our common good. Indeed, the validity of any theory of justice will depend upon the validity of the good it seeks to promote.

That Rawls focused on only one version of teleological theory can be seen in the contrasts he drew between the right and the good. In arguing that agreement on the good of individuals is unnecessary, he wrote that: "Since each person is free to plan his life as he pleases (so long as his intentions are consistent with the principles of justice) unanimity concerning the standards of rationality is not required."[36]

Following in this vein, he noted that a second contrast between the right and the good is confirmed by the judgment that it is a:

> good thing that individuals' conceptions of their good should differ in significant ways, whereas this is not so for conceptions of the right. In a well-ordered society citizens hold the same principles of right and they try to reach the same judgment in particular cases.... [T]here is no urgency to reach a publicly accepted judgment as to what is the good of particular individuals.[37]

While this last statement is true, it ignores the fact that a teleological theory of justice may seek to maximize the good of particular individuals only to the extent that their good is consistent with the common good. For example, Marx's vision of communist society, while lacking any discussion of individual rights, is clearly based on a conception of the common good. If individual rights and obligations are the product of an agreement on the common good, how this good is characterized is of critical importance.

That Rawls appealed to a conception of the common good when he spoke of the priority of the right can also be seen in his equivocation on the meaning of the word "good." He claimed that it is good that individual conceptions of the good differ. Surely, this good cannot be of the same order as the conception of an individual's good. If it were, then while it might be good for Rawls that individual conceptions of the good differ, it need not be good for anyone else. What Rawls seemed to be saying is that it really is good that individual conceptions of their good differ. It is good because variety forms part of his conception of our common good.

It is also worth noting that Rawls did not claim that justice requires individuals to pursue different conceptions of the good. Rather, it is our right to pursue our own ends, within the constraints of justice, because such pursuits conform to a shared conception of the common good. But our conception of the common good is not valid because it conforms to the principles of justice. Rather, the principles of justice are valid only if they conform to a conception of the common good which contractors, seeking to promote their own interests, accept in the original position.

Rawls was correct to say that individual conceptions of the good are constrained by the principles of justice. But it would be incorrect to say that a conception of the common good is limited in this way. In sum, the good for a given individual differs conceptually from a conception of the common good. The common good invokes a common human interest and identity, not identical plans of life.

Rawls described a final contrast between the right and the good in the following way:

> [M]any applications of the principles of justice are restricted by the veil of ignorance, whereas evaluations of a person's good may rely upon a full knowledge of the facts.... A rational plan of life takes into account our special abilities, interests, and circumstances, and therefore it quite properly depends upon our social position and natural assets.[38]

Rawls limited his hypothetical contractors' knowledge of their interests and circumstances in the original position to avoid individual biases in the selection of the principles of justice. This knowledge is fully available, however, when individuals develop their plans of life. What this means is that in adopting principles of justice, we must look to the common good and not to the aggregate good of individuals as endorsed by preference utilitarianism.

Because justice as fairness seeks to promote a conception of our common good, it does not represent a radical departure from the modern teleological views of Marx or Rousseau. Rawls's emphasis on the goods of liberty and equality, for example, is not incompatible with Marx's promotion of self-development and human solidarity.[39] Indeed, individual liberty may be seen as a necessary precondition for self-development and social equality as a pre-condition for the development of human solidarity. In sum, both Marx and Rawls sought to promote goods they believed to be essential to the achievement of human happiness. On this view, individual rights will correspond to those social practices necessary to achieve this goal.[40]

The philosopher Will Kymlicka has also analyzed the purported priority of the right over the good in liberal political theory.[41] In contrast to distinctions drawn by Rawls, Kymlicka has maintained that both the critics and the defenders of liberalism "share the view that principles of right are a spelling out of the requirement that we give equal consideration to each person's good."[42] While equal consideration distinguishes the modern from the ancient tradition, it leaves unresolved the nature of the good to be promoted.

Kymlicka questioned Rawls's conclusion that utilitarians define an act as right because it maximizes the good.[43] According to Rawls, utilitarianism holds that utility maximizing acts are right because they maximize utility. Kymlicka countered that the most compelling and natural form of utilitarianism is not teleological in this sense. Instead, utilitarianism "is a moral theory because it purports to treat people as equals, with equal concern and respect. It does so by counting everyone for one, and no one for more than one....The standard solution is to give each person's interests equal weight."[44]

On this reading, the maximization of utility is not the direct goal of utilitarianism. The goal is equal consideration of each person's preferences. While adopting public measures on the basis of the majority's preferences maximizes utility, its purpose is not utility maximization. Utilitarianism is, therefore, one way of spelling out how our interests are to be given equal consideration. This makes it no less deontological than Rawls's theory. In doing so, utilitarians recognize individuals as having distinct claims.

Rawls regarded utilitarianism to be teleological because it generalizes from the fact that individuals are prudential teleologists. However, Kymlicka has noted that it is simply not the case that utilitarianism fails to distinguish the claims of individuals in the way Rawls maintained.[45] Consequently, the debate between Rawls and utilitarians is not over the priority of the right or the good, but the nature of our common good.

Kynlicka also addressed Rawls's disagreement with the perfectionism of the ancients when he noted that his thin theory of the good may be used to advance many different ways of life. According to Rawls: "[F]ree persons conceive of themselves as beings who can revise and alter their final ends, and who give first priority to preserving their liberty in these matters."[46] For Rawls, individuals have the right to determine what constitutes their particular good. Perfectionist theories, in attempting to impose a conception of the good on the individual, inhibit this process.

Kymlicka argued that Rawls was mistaken in concluding that his dispute with perfectionists was about the priority of the right or the good.[47] According to Kymlicka, perfectionists have a conception of the good life and devise a scheme of distribution which promotes that conception. Rawls had a different conception of the good life which emphasized the liberty to make revisions in individual life plans. According to Kymlicka: "Rawls does not favor the distribution of primary goods out of a concern for the right rather than the good. He simply has a different account of what our good is.... [Rawls and a perfectionist] simply disagree over the nature of the good."[48]

If Kymlicka is correct, then the idea of the right has not supplanted the idea of the good, it has simply redescribed the nature of the good to be promoted. While Rawls was correct in arguing that preference utilitarianism fails to uphold the rights of minorities against the rational preferences of the majority, this objection does not rule out all teleological theories.[49]

If justice as fairness differs from perfectionism only in what it takes to be in our interest, then the debate turns not on the priority of the right or the good, but on competing conceptions of the common good. Social justice will require those measures which best promote a shared conception of our common good; a conception which, while recognizing the fundamental equality of persons, accords to all the liberty to pursue their own vision of the good life.

While social division may block any consensus on the common good, the continuing debate has forever changed much of the modern world. Slavery has been abolished; women have the right to vote; workers have the right to bargain collectively; children are entitled to an education; the disabled to reasonable accommodation. These and many other rights have been obtained through a political struggle between conflicting conceptions of the common good.

This political struggle has produced an egalitarian development within the teleological tradition which promotes both liberty and equality as constitutive of the human good. In addition to the works of Marx and Rousseau, a commitment to social equality is reflected in the works of feminists and communitarians. What unites these theorists is the belief that individual rights can only be determined in light of our social relationships.

While Marx eschewed talk of rights in favor of the good of communist society, Carol Gilligan has written that woman's morality is based not on abstract rights, but on a concern for relationships.[50] Annette Baier has claimed that our concern for the good of human relationships imposes unchosen duties on persons that are not recognized by the rights focus of deontological theory.[51] Indeed, any interest in changing the way men and women interact must look to more than the abstract rights of persons.

Critical legal studies theorist Duncan Kennedy has advanced a conception of the common good in calling for a new legal order based on altruism rather than individualism. According to Kennedy, the conflict between these two norms is a source of indeterminacy in the law.[52]

Fellow legal theorist Roberto Unger has criticized liberal legal practice for ignoring the need for social equality. While acknowledging that the law applies heightened scrutiny to practices which discriminate on the basis of race or gender, Unger has questioned why the same equal protection analysis does not extend to:

> the social division of labor and systematic, discontinuous differentials of access to wealth, power and culture? These inequalities can certainly not be said to be exceptional.... To defend the thesis that racial and sexual advantages count most because they are more severe than other forms of social division and hierarchy would involve the established doctrine in controversies that it could not easily win.[53]

Likewise, communitarians following in the tradition of Aristotle have been critical of the claimed priority of the right. Alasdair MacIntyre, for example, has maintained that the good for persons can be defined only in relation to the good of the community. In disputing the deontological claim that the self is an autonomous chooser of ends, he wrote that:

> We enter human society... with one or more human characters—roles into which we have been drafted—and we have to learn what they are in order to be able to understand how others respond to us and how our responses to them are apt to be construed .... I am never able to seek for the good or exercise the virtues only *qua* individual. I am someone's son or daughter, someone else's cousin or uncle; I am a citizen of this

or that city, a member of this or that guild or profession; I belong to this or that clan, that tribe, this nation. Hence what is good for me has to be the good for one who inhabits these roles. As such I inherit from the past of my family, my city, my tribe, my nation, a variety of debts, inheritances, rightful expectations, and obligations. These constitute the given of my life, my moral starting point.[54]

The conception of the self as embedded in history and constrained by social role sets it apart from the Rawlsian contractors in the original position. On this view, it is impossible to choose principles of justice without explicit knowledge of our interests and circumstances. While Rawls granted his contractors some knowledge of the human condition, his critics have called upon their own knowledge of human nature to reach different conclusions about the common good. These differences are reflected in disagreements about the nature of justice.

In conclusion, I have attempted to show that right is not prior to the good in the way Rawls claimed. Indeed, in the next chapter, I will argue that what distinguishes deontological theories of justice from teleological ones is not the priority of the right, but the primacy of liberty as our most important interest. That is why Rawls and others have insisted on the right of individuals to design their own life plans within the constraints imposed by the principles of justice. The question we must answer is whether individual liberty is in fact primary, or whether social equality is an equal component of our common good. If it is, then the pursuit of happiness will require us to carefully consider our principles of justice.

It is not enough to show that hypothetical contractors would adopt certain principles under specified conditions unless those conditions accurately reflect our actual circumstances. The common good that is to be secured by principles of justice must be of value to all persons. An inaccurate description of such a good will result in an inadequate theory of justice.

A better formulation of the priority of the right may be the priority of the common good. As we have seen, preference utilitarianism concurs with the deontological judgment that the individual is to be the sole judge of his own happiness. Rawls's critique succeeds against preference utilitarianism, not because he accords priority to the right, but because preference utilitarianism fails to adopt a conception of our common good which rules out some preferences as unworthy of consideration.

It is for this reason that neither Plato nor Aristotle could have embraced utilitarianism. For them, justice was not a matter of giving people what they want, but rather what they deserve. On this point, Rawls would agree.

Rawls's thin theory of the good emphasizes our liberty to select and to revise our plans of life. He deemed this liberty to be desirable to all persons regardless of the plans they choose. However, liberty is not the only important good. Equality under the law is also a goal of justice as fairness and of liberal political theory in general. Indeed, Rawls notes that a person's feeling of self-respect requires treatment as an equal.

However, the goal of social equality may be impossible to achieve in class society where the liberty of the few to own the means of production prevents the many from exercising their liberty to control the product of their labor. More-over, the substantial differences in wealth and power that exist in capitalist society make it more difficult for citizens to engage in self-government or to effectively exercise their civil liberties.

The positive liberty of Rousseau implies a different conception of equality than does the negative liberty of Locke. Like the ancients, Rousseau held that equality among citizens is essential for the cultivation of virtue and civic parti-cipation. In contrast, the negative liberty of the moderns employs a conception of equality that stresses not the right of participation, but the right to be left alone. On this account, liberty and equality have value for persons as indi-viduals, but not as members of a community.

The deontological emphasis on the separateness of persons provides a use-ful critique of preference utilitarianism. However, this critique provides no compelling rationale for social equality. Any argument for equality would seem to require a common interest or identity. Without such an interest or identity, social equality would have a purely instrumental value. We would endorse a system of formal equality only in order to avoid the war of each against all.

The idea of the free market reflects this narrow view of social equality. With its emphasis on reciprocity and the right to contract, the commodity mar-ket requires that one must confer a benefit in order to receive one in return. Parties to a contract possess a formal equality because only equals can bind themselves with their promises.

Marx, however, noted that the right to contract is based on a real inequality. One produces not for the other, but for oneself. One seeks to exact not an equal exchange, but an advantageous one. An equal exchange is often impossible be-cause of disparities in abilities and needs which, as Rawls noted, are morally arbitrary.[55] For Marx, the purported equality of the market is replaced by the dictum: "From each according to his ability, to each according to his need." This principle of exchange would establish true equality by making the needs of others as important as our own needs.

In sum, it would seem that the goal of social equality would be better served by an argument based on a common identity. The commonality of family membership generates equality among siblings while imposing obligations on parents and children alike. Political theorists might argue for social equality on the basis of our membership in the human family. Indeed, Marxist, feminist and communitarian critiques of liberalism stress relationships between persons as the basis for social equality.

In this chapter, the difference between the ancient and the modern world views has been characterized in terms of two features: a common human identity and good, and the equality of persons. The combination of these features provides a description of four distinct types of political society which are charted below:

	Inequality	Equality
No common identity	Despotism	Liberal democracy
Common identity	Aristocracy	Communism

Under a despotic government, there is neither a common good or identity, nor any equality between ruler and ruled. Nor does a despot assume the obligation to act in the interests of the ruled. Thus, most would agree that this is the worst form of political organization.

Under an aristocracy or constitutional monarchy, there is still a division between ruler and ruled, but the ruler is obligated to promote the good of his citizens. This form of government represents the idea of the good adopted by the ancients. It would invoke state power to curtail liberty where necessary to promote public morality and the social good. Today, such a view might be endorsed by legal moralists.

In liberal, representative democracies, the people are said to rule themselves. Equal rights are accorded to all citizens and the government is required to remain neutral with respect to competing conceptions of the good. Although principles of justice are supported by an appeal to the common good, this good is defined negatively as the liberty of persons to pursue their own conceptions of the good. Thus, the state has little role to play in the moral education of its citizens.

In communist society, as Marx envisioned it, there would be no state apparatus, so there could be no division between ruler and ruled. There is, however, a conception of the common good which guides individuals in their relations with each other. This conception abolishes divisions based on class and provides for the equal liberty of persons to shape social institutions to promote the good of all.

The philosopher Georg Hegel characterized the development of political society from the state where one is free to the state where all are free. Marx adopted this sequence, but argued that all are free only when the state itself is abolished, and with it, the circumstances of justice. As we shall see in subsequent chapters, Marx's vision of communist society requires a conception of a common good and a common human identity. In providing this conception, there is a reconciliation between the values of liberty and equality and between the good of the individual and the good of society.

Chapter 4

The Priority of Liberty

As we have seen, the contrast between deontological and teleological theories of justice does not turn on the priority of the right or the good, but on the nature of our common good. In this chapter, I contend that deontological theories, in relying upon a conception of the self as an autonomous chooser of ends, have given too much weight to the value of individual liberty. In contrast, a conception of the self as a species or universal being will give equal weight to the values of liberty and equality. In the end, I will argue that the priority of liberty in Rawls's theory of justice provides an inadequate theoretical basis for the achievement of social justice and human happiness.

John Rawls has authored the most acknowledged deontological theory of justice. As noted in chapter three, he contrasted his theory of justice as fairness with utilitarian theories of justice. His belief that utilitarianism fails to take seriously the separateness of persons convinced Rawls that a theory of justice must take into account the notion that individuals have an inviolability which the welfare of everyone else cannot override.[1] On this matter, Rawls held that:

> [I]f we assume that the correct regulative principle for anything depends on the nature of that thing, and that the plurality of distinct persons with separate systems of ends is an essential feature of human societies, we should not expect the principles of social choice to be utilitarian.[2]

Although his objection to preference utilitarianism was well taken, Rawls adopted a thin theory of the good to account for the principles of justice chosen by hypothetical contractors. As a result, his conception of the right is not prior to all conceptions of the good. Indeed, Rawls acknowledged that two conceptions of the good—the idea of goodness as rationality and the idea of social primary goods—are prior to the idea of the right in justice as fairness. With regard to goodness as rationality, Rawls wrote that:

> All the theory of justice assumes is that, in the thin account of the good, the evident criteria of rational choice are sufficient to explain preference for the primary goods, and that such variations as exist in conceptions of rationality do not affect the principles of justice adopted in the original position.[3]

With regard to the social primary goods, Rawls wrote that rational contractors would seek to guarantee the following goods:1) basic rights and liberties; 2) freedom of movement and free choice of occupation; 3) prerogatives of office and position; 4) income and wealth; and 5) the social bases of self-respect.[4] For Rawls, these goods will be valuable for every plan of life.[5]

While his hypothetical contractors must select principles of justice without knowing their particular circumstances, Rawls maintained that they live in a society subject to moderate scarcity and limited benevolence. He described these conditions in the following way:

> Natural and other resources are not so abundant that schemes of cooperation become superfluous, nor are conditions so harsh that fruitful ventures must inevitably break down. While mutually advantageous arrangements are feasible, the benefits they yield fall short of the demands men put forward.[6]

In addition to what he referred to as the "circumstances of justice," Rawls maintained that while the contractors are not envious of each other, they are nevertheless mutually disinterested. He contended that "[t]he postulate of mutual disinterest in the original position is made to insure that the principles of justice do not depend upon strong assumptions....A conception of justice should not presuppose, then, extensive ties of natural sentiment."[7]

In *A Theory of Justice*, Rawls suggested that the circumstances of justice are universal to all societies. He later maintained that these circumstances describe conditions in liberal democratic states.[8] Throughout the development of justice as fairness, however, Rawls made it clear that he understood human beings to be moral agents who possesses both a sense of justice and the ability to adopt and revise a plan of life. Because he believed that respect for individual autonomy is an ideal latent within the political cultures of liberal, democratic states, he concluded that the members of liberal societies would adopt his two principles of justice in the original position.

Given these initial conditions, Rawls held that the contractors would agree to the following two principles of justice: the principle of the greatest equal liberty and the difference principle. The former requires that "each person is to have an equal right to the most extensive basic liberty compatible with a similar liberty for all."[9] The latter requires that "social and economic inequalities are to be arranged so that they are both: (a) to the greatest benefit of the least advantaged, consistent with the just savings principle, and (b) attached to offices and positions open to all under conditions of fair equality of opportunity."[10]

Rawls believed that contractors would adopt these principles because they will maximize the distribution of the social primary goods described above.[11] Of the social primary goods, he opined that self-respect may be the most important when he wrote:

> [P]erhaps the most important primary good is self-respect.... Without it nothing may seem worth doing, or if some things have value for us, we will lack the will to strive for them.... Therefore the parties in the original position would wish to avoid at almost any cost the social conditions that undermine self-respect.[12]

In addition to accounting for the selection of certain primary goods, Rawls stated that the contractors' ignorance of their actual circumstances will cause them to maximize the condition of the least advantaged in society.[13] He endorsed a "maximin principle" because he believed that a strategy of maximizing the minimum social position is the most rational approach under conditions of uncertainty. Thus, Rawls insisted that the contractors would agree to distribute the social primary goods "equally unless an unequal distribution of any or all of these goods is to the advantage of the least favored."[14]

Finally, because of the likelihood of conflict, Rawls adopted priority rules which provide that the principle of the greatest equal liberty is prior to the difference principle and that the difference principle is prior to the principle of efficiency. According to Rawls: "The principles of justice are to be ranked in lexical order and therefore liberty can be restricted only for the sake of liberty."[15] Because justice as fairness gives liberty priority over equality as a principle of justice, it follows that full equality is a goal that is unlikely to be realized in the Rawlsian state.

In sum, the assumptions governing the selection of principles of justice by Rawls's hypothetical contractors are clearly controversial. These assumptions include a conception of the self which, according to Rawls, "is prior to the ends which are affirmed by it."[16] In addition, Rawls's contractors are self-interested, although not necessarily egoistic.[17] Finally, in adopting the maximin principle, individuals are described as essentially risk-averse.[18]

Michael J. Sandel has characterized the Rawlsian self as "a subject of possession, individuated in advance and given prior to its ends."[19] In contrast, Sandel argued for a conception of the self that is socially embedded, with ends that are discovered rather than chosen.

In his book, *Liberalism and the Limits of Justice*, Sandel maintained that the proclaimed priority of the right in justice as fairness leads to a conception of the self that is radically disembodied.[20] He wrote that: "As long as it is assumed that man is by nature a being who chooses his ends rather than a being, as the ancients conceived him, who discovers his ends, then his fundamental preference must necessarily be for conditions of choice rather than, say, for conditions of self-knowledge."[21]

Sandel also noted that while a conception of the unity of human subjectivity plays a role in the Rawlsian system:

> [I]t is a mistake to accord it equal priority with plurality; it is not essential to our nature in the same way…. The priority of plurality over unity, or the notion of the antecedent individuation of the subject, describes the terms of relation between the self and the other that must obtain for justice to be primary.[22]

Both the priority of plurality over unity and the priority of liberty over equality play a significant role in the development of justice as fairness. This priority clearly calls into question the commitment of liberal political theory to the principle of equality as a fundamental value. Indeed, it is difficult to see how a conception of persons as separate, self-interested, and risk-averse can sustain a serious commitment to social equality. At most, such persons would acknowledge the rights of others as the condition for the recognition of their own rights.

On this view, social equality would have an instrumental value which, behind a veil of ignorance, might exceed the value made possible by social inequality. However, such an account of human nature provides little incentive for actual persons to pursue social equality when it is not in their perceived self-interest to do so. This deficiency may explain why Rawls's theory, despite its richness and depth of analysis, has not played a greater role in bringing about social justice.

Instead of the just society, the vision which emerges from the original position is one of a *modus vivendi*, a state in which individuals acknowledge and respect the rights of others only to the extent that it is in their self-interest to do so. In such a state, true equality and community are never achieved because there is no recognition of any common interest and identity that can harmonize the good of the individual with the good of society. In order to achieve that goal, we must reconsider the identity of the self.

Sandel was correct to note that a Rawlsian self would necessarily prefer goods, such as liberty and opportunity, and income and wealth, that are necessary for it to freely pursue whatever plan of life it chooses. Given the lack of any agreement on the good life, the priority of liberty follows. Community, virtue or equality, on the other hand, are primary values only for persons who do not conceive of themselves as given prior to their ends. Therefore, if one is to reject Rawls's theory of justice, one must also reject the conception of the self upon which it was constructed.

In considering this matter, it is important to decide if it is possible to reconcile the principle of the greatest equal liberty with the difference principle. If these principles are irreconcilable, it will be necessary to adopt different principles if we are to achieve the goals of social justice and human happiness.

In considering the compatibility of Rawls's two principles, it should be noted that the relative value of goods such as liberty and opportunity, and income and wealth will vary from one society to another. In a society with strong egalitarian traditions, personal wealth will have less value than in a highly competitive society. Likewise, the perceived value of liberty and opportunity will be less in an agrarian society than in a technologically advanced one. The value of any these goods, therefore, cannot be viewed as absolute.

Given the fact that most individuals in liberal democratic societies do affirm the values of liberty and opportunity, it is important to inquire which liberties and opportunities are most important. It is one thing to affirm freedom of conscience, movement and occupation and quite another to assert the liberty to own the means of production. If the contractors choose the latter, it is controversial whether this liberty is consistent with an equal liberty for all.

According to Rawls, the most important primary good may be the social bases for self-respect. If so, it is unclear why rational contractors would accept economic inequality even if that inequality increased the income and wealth of the least advantaged. It is again controversial whether social inequality is consistent with the good of self-respect.

Nor is it clear that Rawls's list of social primary goods is sufficiently inclusive. Goods such as civic virtue, self-determination and environmental preservation are arguably of value to rational contractors no matter what plan of life they may adopt. If contractors take these goods to be primary, they might discount the value of income and wealth.

In any event, it is reasonable to believe that rational contractors would adopt principles of justice that improved their chances for happiness. Principles which promote liberty and opportunity, income and wealth and the social bases of self-respect would be selected by contractors in the original position only if such goods would increase the likelihood of happiness.[23] Thus, the adoption of principles of justice necessarily relies upon our self-understanding and knowledge of the possible bases for social cooperation.

Rawls's conception of the self, however, provides little opportunity for any self-understanding. Because the deontological self exists prior to its interaction with others, it is difficult to see how this self could embrace the difference principle for anything more than prudential reasons. Given the priority of liberty and plurality in justice as fairness, it seems unlikely that the adoption of the difference principle will bring about genuine social equality.

The difference principle permits economic inequality only to the extent that it works to the benefit of the least advantaged. Rawls justified unequal distributive shares in order:

> to cover the costs of training and education, to attract individuals to places and associations where they are most needed, and so on.... Variations in wages and income and the perquisites of position are simply to influence these choices so that the end result accords with efficiency and justice."[24]

However, it is difficult to know how much inequality is necessary to accord with efficiency and justice. When Rawls wrote about efficiency, he invoked the idea of Pareto optimality, a condition where a redistribution of resources cannot benefit some without producing disadvantages for others.[25] However, there are many possible distributions which accord with Pareto optimality, most of which do not benefit the least advantaged. Nor is it clear on what basis one might determine that any particular distribution of social goods such as income and wealth will benefit the least advantaged.

In addition to this practical difficulty, it appears that a commitment to economic efficiency within a framework of private ownership of the means of production would maintain a permanent inequality. That economic inequality is a permanent feature of capitalist societies is illustrated by the following example.

Restricting our inquiry to economic values, the difference principle requires income redistribution through progressive taxation and transfer payments up to the point where further taxation would worsen the condition of the least advantaged. Given the profit motive at work in capitalism, every effort to redistribute income will eventually reduce the incentives for private risk-taking necessary for the production of wealth. The resulting decrease in investment will reduce the total wealth available for redistribution. At this point, further progressivity in tax rates will worsen the economic condition of the least advantaged. Thus, as long as economic resources are privately owned, the difference principle will require economic inequality. Given the importance of material values in capitalist society, the permanent economic inequality required by the difference principle is likely to ensure permanent social and political inequality as well.

If one considers the full range of the social primary goods, however, it may be impossible to know when an unequal distribution of income and wealth will benefit the least advantaged. Such a determination would require both a definition of the least advantaged group and a description of its interests in relation to the full range of social primary goods.

If, on the other hand, one defines the least advantaged group solely in terms of income and wealth, then contractors would endorse an unequal distribution of these goods only if it produced more income and wealth for the poorest members of society. On this view, capitalist economic inequality would be preferable to socialist economic equality if the members of the poorest class in capitalist society were wealthier than they would be in socialist society. However, this answer would suffice, despite its practical difficulties, only if one ignores the distribution of other social primary goods.

Because rational contractors would endorse goods other than income and wealth, it would be incorrect to define the least advantaged group solely in these terms. An unequal distribution of income, even if it maximized the income of the poorest members of society, might not satisfy the difference principle, because it might not benefit the members of the least advantaged group with respect to other social primary goods. Indeed, it would be impossible to know who is among the least advantaged unless it can be known how any possible distribution affects the interests of those individuals in terms of the entire list of social primary goods. In practice, such a determination seems impossible.

The impracticality of this project becomes even clearer if one is willing to expand the list of social primary goods. For example, if goods such as self-determination or environmental preservation are deemed to be primary, there would be situations where it would be impossible to benefit the least advantaged. Consider, for example, the debate over logging in our national forests. If one acknowledges that both income and wealth, on the one hand, and environmental preservation, on the other, constitute social primary goods, then any decision about logging would reduce one of these primary goods. Even where there is agreement that development and preservation are both essential to the realization of individual life plans, an appeal to the difference principle will not resolve the dispute because any decision will be to the disadvantage of some least advantaged group.[26] When a social decision requires a choice between two or more competing primary goods, then the least advantaged group will be the one whose good is not promoted. As a result, the difference principle can provide no determinate answer to resolve the conflict.

In practice, such disputes are often resolved by administrative agencies through a utilitarian calculus known as a cost-benefit analysis. However, an approach based on an economic conception of the good may be inappropriate where non-economic values are at stake. Likewise, political decisions based on the will of the majority are equally utilitarian.

Any decision about logging, or a myriad of other public policy issues, must rely upon some conception of the common good. By making income and wealth social primary goods, but not environmental preservation, the application of the difference principle tilts the balance to the side of development. If the proposed development improves the income or wealth of the poorest members of society, it is assumed that they will endorse it. In fact, such an assumption often turns out to be in error.

Thus, it appears that any application of the difference principle requires that no social primary good conflict with any other. But the resulting exclusion of goods such as self-determination and environmental preservation prejudices the difference principle against goods that are essential to many people. Because this exclusion is prejudicial, it is unlikely that rational contractors would accept Rawls's list as complete.

In response, a Rawlsian might argue that his principle of equality of fair opportunity is lexically prior to the difference principle.[27] However, this principle only ensures individual access to positions of responsibility. It says nothing about how public policy should be determined. Nor does it guarantee any right to the shared decision-making necessary to the establishment of social equality.

Failing this, one might argue that the principles of justice only apply to those goods taken to be common by all rational contractors. But this distinction between controversial and non-controversial primary goods seems arbitrary. Simply because some persons do not take environmental preservation or self-determination to be essential to their plan of life does not diminish the importance of these goods for other individuals. If universal assent is required, one could certainly find persons for whom income and wealth do not constitute primary goods. By excluding certain primary goods, justice as fairness distorts the nature of social agreement in the original position.

To this charge, a Rawlsian might respond that justice as fairness is only offered as a means to judge the fairness of the basic institutions of society. Differences in personal preferences can be resolved through market mechanisms. For example, if the pristine quality of the wilderness is important to environmentalists, they may buy the development rights from those who own them or, in the case of government ownership, the land could be auctioned off to the highest bidder.

What this solution ignores is the fact that what persons are willing or able to pay is not a true measure of the value of a public resource. For example, individuals who purchase a resource for preservation purposes do not derive the same type of benefit as do those who purchase it for development. Unlike private development, the preservation of a public resource provides the same non-economic value for all persons who prize this good while the private development of a resource provides the developer with a far greater share of the economic value. Any auction scheme would distort the value of a resource in favor of its development.[28]

Moreover, why should the equitable distribution of social goods be limited to those goods endorsed by all? Even if one believes that income and wealth are primary goods, there are surely situations where most persons would prefer values other than additional income or wealth. In such cases, increasing income and wealth at the expense of a competing value would not improve the situation of the least advantaged.[29]

For the reasons provided above, it will be difficult to resolve distributional issues with the difference principle because there is no certain way to know when inequality actually benefits the least advantaged in society. Even if we define the least advantaged solely in terms of economic values, some members of the least advantaged group will prefer values other than the economic benefits made possible by economic inequality.

In addition to the application problems described above, there is also a question of the lexical priority of the principle of the greatest equal liberty. Why should we favor individual liberty over the satisfaction of basic human needs? One might reply that the Kantian ideal of individual autonomy places a greater premium on basic civil liberties. But there is a problem with this position. Welfare provisions under the difference principle restrict the liberty of persons to retain the product of their efforts. According to libertarians, the extensive redistribution of wealth required by justice as fairness undermines the system of basic liberties if one takes seriously the right of property ownership.

This problem with justice as fairness lies at the heart of Robert Nozick's conservative critique of *A Theory of Justice*.[30] In contrast to Rawls, Nozick has proposed a theory in which individuals are entitled to retain or transfer property which has been justly acquired. While justice as fairness affirms the right of individuals to pursue their own conceptions of the good, Nozick contends that Rawls's theory does not provide them with an effective means to do so. He wrote that:

> The man who chooses to work longer to gain an income more than sufficient for his basic needs prefers some extra goods or services to the leisure and activities he could perform during the possible non-working hours; whereas the man who chooses not to work the extra time prefers the leisure activities to the extra goods or services he could acquire by working more. Given this, if it would be illegitimate for a tax system to seize some of a man's leisure (forced labor) for the purpose of serving the needy, how can it be legitimate for a tax system to seize some of a man's goods for that purpose?[31]

In equating taxation with forced labor, Nozick argued that a commitment to the difference principle means that a basic liberty has been compromised. His argument is elaborated in an example offered by Alisdair MacIntyre involving hypothetical characters named A and B.[32] "A" has struggled to buy a small house and send his children to college. Because he thinks of justice along the lines of Nozick's entitlement theory, he regards the tax increases required by the difference principle to be an unjust threat to his standard of living. "B" is relatively well off and is more concerned with eliminating inequalities in power and wealth. Because "B" follows Rawls in believing that justice sets limits to legitimate acquisition and entitlement, he supports higher taxes and more income redistribution.

According to MacIntyre, in a pluralistic culture lacking any agreement about entitlements and the common good, it will be impossible to resolve the conflict between "A" and "B" and, for the same reason, between Rawls and Nozick. MacIntyre further maintained that our society "possesses no method of weighing, no rational criterion for deciding between claims based on legitimate entitlement against claims based on need."[33]

The dispute between Rawls and Nozick would seem, therefore, to turn on the status of private property in liberal democracies. The private ownership of the means of production might be justified on either one of two grounds. Private ownership is either a basic right of persons or it is the most efficient means to promote the common good. If a Rawlsian invokes the first justification, he must explain why the owners of productive enterprises must share the wealth generated by those enterprises. Why should a basic liberty be compromised under a system that advocates the priority of liberty?

In *A Theory of Justice*, Rawls attempted to answer this question by rejecting the idea that individuals have a pre-institutional right to any particular distributional share.[34] Instead, he held that morally arbitrary differences in natural talents and social circumstance should not give rise to entitlements because they are not the products of individual choice.

However, this answer would not persuade Nozick or a person like "A" in MacIntyre's example who believes that someone who works longer or harder than someone else is entitled to the additional income he earns. "A" would certainly question why it is necessary that the least advantaged must benefit before he can lay claim to his wages. While differences in natural abilities and social position may be arbitrary, differences in effort are generally within an individual's control. Justice as fairness, however, supports pay differentials only if they will benefit the least advantaged. This position seems to ignore the reasonable desire of contractors to retain control over the means to satisfy their plans of life.

If, on the other hand, private ownership of the means of production is justified on efficiency grounds, we are back to the problem of reconciling competing conceptions of the common good. Private ownership may be justified only if it can be shown to maximize the value of the social primary goods for the least advantaged members of society. The validity of such a claim is far from self-evident. Not only should we not presume that private ownership has increased the income and wealth of the least advantaged, there is reason to believe that rational contractors might prefer values such as self-determination and health and safety in the workplace over greater income and wealth.

In sum, if private ownership is justified as a basic liberty, the massive redistribution of income required by the difference principle will conflict with the principle of the greatest equal liberty. If private ownership is justified as the most efficient means to promote the common good, one must explain why the goods of income and wealth outweigh competing goods such as health and safety and self-determination. One must also consider whether a reduction of these goods is consistent with the need to preserve the social bases of self-respect.

As these comments suggest, justice as fairness has been attacked from both the left and the right. Egalitarian critics have questioned the compatibility of private ownership with both the difference principle and the principle of the greatest equal liberty. Private ownership would satisfy Rawls's first principle only if the opportunity for ownership is equal for all persons.[35] But as G.A. Cohen has pointed out, while it is possible for an individual worker to become a capitalist, it is not possible for the entire working class to become capitalists.[36] Were the latter to occur, there would be no one left to perform the requisite labor.

This consequence raises the issue of whether the right to employ others is a liberty that is equal for all. In Cohen's opinion, it is an equal liberty only if the majority fails to exercise it. Thus, if private ownership of the means of production is to be considered a basic liberty, it must be of a different nature than the freedom of speech or religion where the exercise by some does not necessarily inhibit the exercise by others.

The liberty to own the means of production does resemble one basic liberty—the right to choose one's occupation. A person is free to become a lawyer or a laborer without that choice restricting the options of others. However, the liberty to own the means of production differs from the liberty to be a lawyer in an important sense. The person who is unable to pursue a career in law because of overcrowding is free to pursue a career in other fields. A person who lacks the capital to own a productive enterprise has no similar alternative. There is no other option but to work, starve, or live off the income of others. The private ownership of the means of production requires not only that the ranks of the capitalist class be limited, but that the ranks of the working class be large. In this regard, the liberty to own the means of production cannot be equal for all.

This analysis of the unfreedom of the working class is reflected in what Jeffrey Reiman has called "structural force" under capitalism. Reiman pointed out that workers are forced to sell their labor power because they lack any acceptable alternatives.[37] This force seems to be invisible because there is no particular capitalist who forces any particular worker to labor for him. In fact, people appear to freely sell their labor power in return for a wage. Reiman wrote that:

When Marx wrote that the wage-worker "is compelled to sell himself of his own free will" (*Capital I*, p. 766), he was not being arch or paradoxical. He was telling us both how force works in capitalism and why it is unseen.... [W]hat Marxists call capitalist ideology boils down to little more than the invisibility of structural force.[38]

At this point, one might ask why this situation is troubling. After all, many professional employees enjoy rewarding careers and exercise considerable autonomy in their work lives. However, the focus of that argument is misplaced. Support for a capitalist division of labor should not take the perspective of the most advantaged members of the working class, but should consider the well-being of the least advantaged.

At the bottom of the employment ladder are none of the perquisites or prestige enjoyed by professional employees. Here are persons who receive low wages for often dangerous and unhealthy work, with little opportunity for advancement and little respect from their employers or society at large. Their grievances are often ignored and, given the structural unemployment of capitalist economies, their employment status is far from secure. Indeed, entire plants may be closed when the wage demands of the local workforce exceed those of workers elsewhere.

The lack of autonomy in the workplace is addressed in Marx's critique of alienated labor summarized in chapter 2 of this work. This critique demonstrates the impoverishment of the right to sell one's labor power in a free market. The critique of alienated labor presents a problem for the defenders of capitalism because alienation is an evil which cannot be eliminated through the payment of wages. The evil results not from the fact that workers are not paid the full value of their labor power, but because they lose control of the labor process.

Nor can alienated labor be justified even if the community is richer because of a capitalist division of labor. In such a situation, the individual worker is sacrificed when labor, his life activity, is controlled by another. Rawls was justifiably critical of preference utilitarianism because of its willingness to sacrifice the good of an individual for the good of the community. However, if a person's good is linked to his productive life, then the capitalist division of labor is guilty of the same violation.

Liberal political theory has largely ignored the critique of alienated labor based on the assumption that the labor contract is freely chosen. But the observations of Cohen and Reiman undermine this assumption. If workers do not freely choose their positions because they are coerced by a false necessity, then the private ownership of the means of production is inconsistent with any principle of justice which takes seriously the social bases of self-respect.[39] In light of Marx's critique of alienated labor, there is reason to believe that rational contractors would not endorse a capitalist economic system. Under a maximin strategy, it would be reasonable to insist on the right to actively participate in economic decision-making.

In conclusion, the success of justice as fairness requires that hypothetical contractors agree about the goods they hold in common. However, it is insufficient to show what contractors would agree to under specified conditions if those conditions do not accurately reflect the truth about human nature. Are individuals mutually disinterested? Is the self given prior to its ends? If these and other assumptions are invalid, then the selection of the social primary goods and the principles of justice will not lead to social justice or human happiness.

In contrast to Rawls, political theorists such as Sandel and MacIntyre deny that the self is given prior to its ends. They describe a self that is embedded in history and society, with many commitments that are unchosen. This feature of social life makes the priority of liberty not only a false ideal, but an impediment to the development of true community.

The questions posed above suggest that further inquiry into the nature the self is necessary. This inquiry leads us to Marx's conception of the self as a species being.

Chapter 5

Self-Identity and Species Being

In chapters one and two, we examined Marcuse's claim that human happiness requires material abundance, social justice and self-knowledge. In chapters three and four, we saw that the contrast between deontological and teleological theories of justice does not turn on the priority of the right or the good, but on competing conceptions of the common good. Moreover, deontological theories of justice have endorsed the priority of liberty over equality because they rely upon a conception of the self as an autonomous chooser of ends. Teleological theories have promoted goods such as virtue or equality, based on a conception of the self that is socially embedded.

In the final three chapters, I will explore a conception of the self that may help to reconcile the competing claims of liberty and equality, individualism and community. In building upon Marx's description of the self as a species being, this discussion will seek to clarify the nature of the self and the principles of justice necessary to produce a general happiness.

Let us suppose an agreement on a social ideal between the supporters of equality and the supporters of liberty. For the sake of simplicity, we may designate these groups as liberals and conservatives. Suppose that both groups would endorse a system of social cooperation in which individuals are free to pursue their own conceptions of the good life. Liberty is preserved because no one exercises arbitrary authority over anyone else, while equality is preserved because no one is denied the means to satisfy his needs.

While it is possible to imagine agreement on this ideal, there has been no agreement on the means to achieve it. The conservative emphasis on liberty requires an extensive system of individual rights while the liberal concern for equality has imposed significant limitations on the exercise of individual liberty.

Conservatives insist on the right to be free from governmental interference and the right to retain the product of their labor. On this view, liberty can be achieved only when the market represents the chief instrument of distribution. Only on the basis of voluntary exchange will persons be able to establish the bases for social cooperation.

Liberals, on the other hand, are suspicious of free markets and often reject the rights prized by conservatives. In their view, equality demands an active state apparatus to eliminate the vestiges of a class system. Until genuine social cooperation is achieved, only the state can ensure a fair distribution of goods and services.

This difference in orientation underlies our difficulty in achieving social cooperation. While both the conservative and the liberal value cooperation, one demands liberty as its basis while the other insists on equality. The conservative prizes liberty because he conceives the self to be an autonomous chooser of ends while the liberal prizes equality because he sees the self as the product of social interaction.

What we must consider is whether there is a way to reconcile these two conceptions of the self and the disparate principles of justice they support. Is there an answer to the riddle Rousseau posed as the problem for political theory: How to form a society which promotes the welfare of all by means of which each person, while uniting with all, obeys only himself and remains as free as before?

The solution to this riddle requires a closer examination of the self. Marx's conception of the self as a species being offers one solution to Rousseau's riddle. Although this conception distinguishes human beings from other species, it supports a common human identity that transcends race, religion, nation, class or gender. This common identity will be necessary to reconcile the divisions within class society. In order to resolve the division between humankind and the rest of the nature, we will need an even broader conception of the self.

Marx's analysis of the self as a creative universal being was discussed in chapter 2. Unfortunately, the conception of the self as a species being has been misunderstood by some of his critics. In an article entitled "Reconsidering Historical Materialism," G.A. Cohen criticized Marx's philosophical anthropology for its "severe one-sidedness".[1] Cohen's criticism is important because it is shared by many who characterize Marx's early writings as hopelessly utopian.

Cohen argued that "Marx went too far in the materialist direction" with his "exclusive emphasis on the creative side of human nature." In doing so, "he failed to do justice to the self's irreducible interest in a definition of itself."[2] Following Hegel, Cohen saw the need for self-identity to include a connection to something outside the self which the self has not created. He maintained that this need explains phenomena for which Marxism is unable to account, such as the enduring attraction of religion and nationalism.

While it is true that self-identity requires a connection to something which the self has not created, it is unlikely that the young Marx would have disagreed with this claim. For the reasons which follow, it does not appear that Marx's philosophical anthropology was as materialistic as Cohen has contended.

According to Cohen, Marx defined the self in terms of its powers or capacities. For Marx, the exercise of essential human powers affirms human nature by objectifying our nature in the products we create. For Cohen, however, self-definition must do more than this. He wrote that a person "needs to know who he is, and how his identity connects him with particular others."[3]

For Cohen, Marx's blindness to the importance of self-identity led him to underestimate social divisions based on religion, gender, race and nationality. He concluded that Marx's antagonism to social roles "reflects a failure to appreciate how the very constraints of role can help to link a person with others in satisfying community."[4]

In support of his charge of one-sidedness, Cohen cited Marx's passage in *The German Ideology* that "in communist society there are no painters but at most people who engage in painting among other activities."[5] Cohen took this passage to imply two facts about communism: that no one will paint full-time and that no one will assume the social role of a painter. Cohen argued that the inability to assume social roles would inhibit the development of a person's self-identity.

An examination of the context of Marx's statement, however, suggests an alternative reading. First of all, the statement is part of a longer critique of the views of Max Stirner. Stirner had distinguished the unique labor of great artists from mere human labor and had held that the former could not be socialized. In response, Marx wrote: "[I]t was not their [the communists'] view, as Sancho [Stirner] imagines, that each should do the work of Raphael, but that in anyone in whom there is a potential Raphael should be able to develop without hindrance."[6]

Marx went on to point out that Raphael's work was conditioned by the division of labor in effect at the time. He wrote that: "Raphael as much as any other artist was determined by the technical advances made in art before him, by the organisation of society and the division of labour in his locality, and, finally, by the division of labour in all the countries with which his locality had intercourse."[7]

Marx was critical of the division of labor because of the limitations it imposed on the development of individual talents. His preference for communism derived from his observation that:

> The exclusive concentration of artistic talent in particular individuals, and its suppression in the broad mass which is bound up with this, is a consequence of division

of labour.... [W]ith a communist organisation of society, there disappears the subordination of the artist to local and national narrowness, which arises entirely from division of labour, and also the subordination of the individual to some definite art, making him exclusively a painter, sculptor, etc.; the very name expresses the narrowness of his professional development and his dependence on division of labour. In a communist society there are no painters but only people who engage in painting among other activities.[8]

In this passage, Marx's intent seems twofold. First, he criticized the artificial division between human and unique labor by showing that even unique artistic endeavor is subject to the division of labor. Second, he argued for the end of that division as the means to free persons from a system of socially imposed roles. What Marx objected to was a system which makes one person *exclusively* a painter, another a sculptor and so on. While individuals would be free to be more than just a painter or a sculptor in communist society, there is no reason to believe that they would be prevented from painting full-time.

This interpretation of Marx finds support in a famous passage in which he described life under communism. In the following passage, Marx did not seem concerned with social roles *per se* but with their forced character under a capitalist division of labor. He wrote:

And finally, the division of labour offers us the first example of how, as long as man remains in natural society, that is, as long as a cleavage exists between the particular and the common interest, as long, therefore, as activity is not voluntarily, but naturally divided, man's own deed becomes an alien power opposed to him, which enslaves him instead of being controlled by him. For as soon as the distribution of labor comes into being, each man has a particular exclusive sphere of activity, which is forced upon him and which he cannot escape. He is a hunter, a fisherman, a shepherd, or a critical critic, and must remain so if he does not want to lose his means of livelihood; while in communist society, where nobody has one exclusive sphere of activity but each can become accomplished in any branch he wishes, society regulates the general production and thus makes it possible for me to do one thing today and another tomorrow, to hunt in the morning, fish in the afternoon, criticise after dinner, just as I have a mind, without ever becoming hunter, fisherman, shepherd or critic.[9]

Marx made several points in this passage. Under a division of labor in which our particular and our common interests do not coincide, human beings are forced to accept exclusive social roles. Under communism, however, individuals would be free to pursue any activity they choose. Rather than a rejection of social roles, Marx's statement should be read as an indictment of socially imposed roles. He wrote that communism makes it *possible* for an individual to do one thing today and another tomorrow, not that he will be *required* to do so.

Moreover, it did not matter to Marx if a person who painted part-time thought of himself as a painter while a person who painted full-time did not. How individuals choose to define themselves was not the point of the passage. The point was that under communism personal choice will determine a person's life activity and self-definition. There is no suggestion that anyone will be compelled or prevented from defining himself in a particular way. Indeed, in a stateless society, there would be no mechanism of compulsion.

Closely related to the charge that Marx would abolish social roles is Cohen's assertion that Marx called for the "free and full" development of *all* of a person's abilities. While such a development would be physically im-possible, Cohen stated that this "absurd" view must be attributed to Marx because he "so often speaks of the individual developing *all* of his powers."[10] Furthermore, Cohen argued that there is a connection between Marx's materialism and his demand for the total development of the individual when he wrote:

> I do think, even if I cannot show, that the materialism encourages the wish to draw forth everything in the individual, and I note that no corresponding error is naturally associated with an emphasis on the importance of self definition. There is no temptation to think that one has a satisfactory identity only when one identifies with everything that can be identified with.[11]

In this passage , Cohen contrasted his conception of self-definition with what he understood to be Marx's concern for the full and free development of all of a person's abilities. Given the principle of interpretive charity, it would be a mistake to hold Marx to a physically impossible goal unless the textual evidence supports no other interpretation. Exactly what evidence did Cohen advance for attributing such a goal to Marx?

Cohen cited a passage from *The German Ideology* in which Marx wrote: "[F]ree activity is for the communists the creative manifestation of life arising from the free development of all abilities."[12] An examination of the context provides grounds for a competing interpretation. Again, the statement is contained in a longer response to Stirner. This time, Stirner proposed a new theory of exploitation in which workers in a factory are said to exploit each other because each worker is only able to perform one piece of work. According to Stirner, all work should have the aim of satisfying "Man". Man is not satisfied unless the individual is able to perform work in its totality.[13]

Marx ridiculed Stirner's analysis of human ability when he wrote that: "'Man' remains a maker of pinheads, but he has the consolation of knowing that the pinhead is part of the pin and that he is able to make the whole pin."[14]

For Marx, Stirner's concern for "Man" was wrong for two reasons. First, the free development of human abilities requires its actual expression. It is not enough to know that one is able to do something. Second, by equating the communists' "free activity" with "dull labour," Stirner drew a false distinction between physical activity and the "hard work of thought." It was this distinction between mental and physical labor and the denigration of the latter that Marx found objectionable.

For Marx, the free development of "all" of a person's abilities in this context can be plausibly said to refer to the development of both mental and physical abilities. Under communism, human beings would be free to develop both mental and physical abilities rather than being limited to the development of one set at the expense of the other. Stirner's "Man" was free because he knew he could make the whole pin. For Marx, real freedom lies not in knowledge alone, but in the ability to use that knowledge to act in freedom.

Continuing on this point, Cohen asked the reader to consider the phrase "the free development of the individual as a whole" and its context.[15] When one considers the context of *The German Ideology*, however, several important facts are revealed. One, the editor of the work noted that the passage Cohen cited had been crossed out in Marx's manuscript. In addition, the word "ability" does not appear in the passage. Instead, Marx seemed to be concerned with the satisfaction of human needs and desires. The passage in which the phrase "the free development of the individual as a whole" is found reads as follows:

> The fact that one desire of an individual in modern society can be satisfied at the expense of all others, and that this "ought not to be" and that this is more or less the case with all individuals in the world today and that thereby the free development of the individual as a whole is made impossible—this fact is expressed by Stirner thus: "the desires become fixed" in the egoist in disagreement with himself.... The communists have no intention of abolishing the fixedness of their desires and needs... they only strive to achieve an organisation of production and intercourse which will make possible the normal satisfaction of all needs, ie. a satisfaction which is limited only by the needs themselves.[16]

What are we to make of this passage? In it, Marx bemoaned the fact that in modern society one human desire can be satisfied only at the expense of other desires. For the worker, the desire for the means to life can be satisfied only by labor in service to another. According to Marx, alienated labor is "not the satisfaction of a need; it is merely a means to satisfy needs external to it."[17]

The free development of the individual as a whole is impossible under capitalism because the desire for the means to life can be satisfied only by the denial of other desires. Communist society would remedy this situation by making possible the satisfaction of all of a person's needs. There is no hint that individuals in communist society would be encouraged to develop new needs which could be satisfied only by developing *all* of their abilities. Thus, "the free development of the individual as a whole" cannot mean what Cohen has asserted.

If Cohen's interpretation on this point is incorrect, what might Marx have meant when he called for the "free and full development"of all human abilities? Given the context, it is clear that Marx opposed the one-sided development of abilities required by a capitalist division of labor. Moreover, he opposed the exclusivity of social roles in capitalist society because individuals are free to develop some abilities only at the expense of other ones.

In sum, it would be wrong to say that Marx opposed all social roles. What he opposed was the forced character of exclusive social roles that restrict the development of human abilities. He called for a society in which individuals would be free to develop *any* of their abilities and to satisfy *all* of their needs as opposed to one in which persons are only allowed to develop *some* of their abilities and to satisfy *some* of their needs. Marx certainly knew that it was impossible for human beings to fully develop all of their abilities. For that reason, any interpretation which attributes such a position to Marx should be rejected unless the evidence makes no other interpretation possible.

The question of social roles and the development of human abilities signals a further point in Cohen's rejection of Marx's philosophical anthropology. In "The Dialectic of Labour in Marx," Cohen argued that Marx's vision of communism represents not a form of society, but an alternative to it. He wrote:

> The abolition of roles may be... nonsense, but it is an idea we find in Marx.... He wanted individuals to face one another and themselves without mediation of institutions....It is no great exaggeration to say that Marx's freely associated individuals constitute an alternative to, not a form of, society."[18]

But surely it is an exaggeration. For as soon as freely associated individuals agree to regulate communal production an institution is born. Indeed, the transition from socialism to communism would be impossible without the coordination of institutions on a grand scale. In any event, it would be fair to say that democratic decision-making requires democratic institutions under any conception of "free association." Thus, Marx's freely associated individuals would not be wholly individualistic.

Cohen, however, did not stop here. In "Reconsidering Historical Materialism," he further claimed that Marx took the position that society is required only as a means to an independently specified goal. That goal is the free and full development of all human powers. Cohen wrote:

> It is true that for Marx the liberation of the human material is possible only in community with others since 'only within the community has each individual the means of cultivating his gifts in all directions', but here society is required, as Marx puts it, as a *means*, to an independently specified (and I argued, absurd) goal. It is not required, less instrumentally, as a field for that self-identification the need for which is unnoticed in Marx's vitalistic formulations.[19]

Here, Cohen made two claims. He asserted that in viewing society only as a means for the development of human powers, Marx did not believe that human beings are essentially social. This reading is required by his claim that Marx promoted communism as an alternative to society. In addition, Cohen suggested that Marx failed to take seriously the human need for self-identity.[20] Neither of these claims rings true.

When examined in context, the statement that "only within the community has each individual the means of cultivating his gifts in all directions," does not support Cohen's criticism. In the paragraph in which this excerpt appeared, Marx stated that:

> The transformation, through the division of labor, of personal powers (relations) into material powers, cannot be dispelled by dismissing the general idea of it from one's mind, but can only be abolished by the individuals again subjecting these material powers to themselves and abolishing the division of labour. This is not possible without community. Only within the community has the individual the means of cultivating his gifts in all directions; hence personal freedom becomes possible only within the community. In the previous substitutes for the community, in the state, etc., personal freedom has existed only for the individuals who developed under the conditions of the ruling class. The illusory community in which individuals have up till now combined

always took on an independent existence in relation to them, and since it was the combination of one class over against another, it was at the same time for the oppressed class not only a completely illusory community, but a new fetter as well. In the real community the individuals obtain their freedom in and through their association.[21]

Not only does this passage not support the instrumentalist interpretation offered by Cohen, it supports the view that Marx saw human beings as essentially social. If community is merely the means for individual development, then what motivated Marx's distinction between real and illusory community? Why did he write that individuals obtain their freedom in and through their association? Marx distinguished real from illusory community because only in real community do persons affirm their identity as species beings. Only in real community is the freedom of one not dependent upon the servitude of another.

Marx's interest in the development of real community was consistent with his characterization of the self as a species being. In the *Economic and Philosophic Manuscripts of 1844*, he wrote that:

The human essence of nature first exists only for social man; for only here does nature exist for him as a bond with man—as his existence for the other and the other's existence for him—as the life element of the human world; only here does nature exist as the foundation of his own human existence.... What is to be avoided above all is the reestablishing of "Society" as an abstraction *vis a vis* the individual. The individual is the social being. His life... is therefore an expression and confirmation of social life.[22]

It would be a mistake to judge Marx's characterization of human nature as simply creative. For Marx, human beings are both creative and social by nature. This dual character was ignored by Cohen when he wrote that communist society is merely the means for the satisfaction of individual ends.

The inadequacy of Cohen's characterization of Marx's philosophical anthropology can be seen in another way. For if the free and full development of human powers was all that Marx was after, it is unclear why he would prefer communism to a system of simple commodity production. In the latter, there would no exploitation as that term was used by Marx to describe the extraction of surplus labor.[23]

However, Marx criticized the simple exchange of Lockean producers in this passage in the *Manuscripts*:

As soon as exchange occurs, there is an overproduction beyond the immediate boundary of ownership. But this overproduction does not exceed selfish need. Rather it is only an indirect way of satisfying a need which finds its objectification in the production of another person.... I have produced for myself and not for you, just as you have produced for yourself and not for me.... No one is gratified by the product of another. Our mutual production means nothing to us as human beings.... Human nature is not the bond of our production for each other.....Each of us sees in his product only his own objectified self-interest which is independent, alien, and objectified. As a human being, however, you do have a human relation to my product. It is the object of your desire and your will.... My social relationship with you and my labor for your want is just plain deception..... Mutual pillaging is at its base.[24]

This passage confirms that, for Marx, alienation divides human beings not only from their productive powers, but also from each other as species beings. As long as I produce for myself and not for you, and you produce for yourself and not for me, our common identity is unrealized. While simple commodity production does not directly exploit human labor power, it is inconsistent with a world in which human beings act in concert for a common good. This emphasis on the common good was essential for Marx because human identity is common. Real community is not only the means for human fulfillment. It is human fulfillment.

In conclusion, there is nothing in Marx's philosophical anthropology which demands the full development of every human ability. Because human beings are both social and creative by nature, real community will make it possible for individuals to freely develop their abilities without interference and to fully satisfy their needs, including the need for community. For Marx, the achievement of communism did not require the abolition of social roles. Rather, it would free individuals from the exclusive roles imposed by a capitalist division of labor. In abolishing that division of labor, communism would make possible the development of the whole person. Far from being a mere means to the development of human powers, communist society represented, for Marx, the fulfillment of our species being.

In rejecting Marx's philosophical anthropology, Cohen did raise the important issue of self-identity. He noted that nations and religious communities play an important role in this process because "[i]n adhering to traditionally defined collectivities people retain a sense of who they are."[25]

According to Cohen: "A person does not only need to develop and enjoy his powers. He needs to know who he is, and how his identity connects him with particular others. He must, as Hegel saw, find something outside himself which he did not create, and to which something inside himself corresponds."[26]

Cohen considered Marx's conception of human nature to be one-sided because it focused on the development of human abilities while ignoring the need for self-understanding. He argued that his conception represents an improvement because there is no corresponding likelihood of equating a satisfying identity "only when one identifies with everything that can be identified with."[27] As we have seen, however, Cohen's charge of one-sidedness makes sense only if Marx did not consider human beings to be social by nature. Because this characterization appears to be incorrect, the conception of the self as a species being does respond to Cohen's concern for self-identity.[28]

In fact, Marx's conception of the self as a species being provides an important account of self-identity. In distinguishing human from non-human species he observed that:

> The animal is immediately identical with its life-activity. It does not distinguish itself from it. It is its life-activity. Man makes his life-activity itself the object of his will and of his consciousness.... In creating an objective world by his practical activity, in working up inorganic nature, man proves himself a conscious species being, ie., as a being that treats the species as its own essential being, or that treats itself as a species being....[A]n animal only produces what it immediately needs for itself or its young. It produces one-sidedly, whilst man produces universally.[29]

For Marx, we are not only creative, we are conscious of ourselves as creative. We are also conscious of ourselves as members of a species which shares creative powers. The importance of self-consciousness is emphasized by a famous passage in *Capital*:

> By thus acting on the external world and changing it, [man] at the same time changes his own nature. He develops his slumbering powers and compels them to act in obedience to his sway.... A spider conducts operations that resemble those of a weaver, and a bee puts to shame many an architect in the construction of her cells. But what distinguishes the worst architect from the best of bees is this, that the architect raises the structure in his imagination before he erects it in reality. At the end of every labour process, we get a result that already existed in the imagination of the labourer at its commencement.[30]

What did Marx mean when he wrote that man changes his nature? In the *Theses on Feuerbach*, he stated that "the human essence is... the ensemble of the social relations."[31] If Marx identified human nature as both changing and as the ensemble of social relations, then he must have had in mind something more than creativity and social being. For human beings have been both social and creative under every mode of production.

The aspect of human nature which changes along with changes in the relations of production is our self-consciousness. Marx distinguished human beings from other animals because we are conscious of our ourselves as species beings. Therefore, when we change our nature as a result of our labor, what has changed is not our creative or social nature, but our consciousness of our nature. In changing our consciousness, we confirm our identity as species beings. According to both Marx and Marcuse, this change in consciousness brings with it new needs which cannot be satisfied in class societies. It is this change in the structure of our needs which will lead to changes in the basic institutions of society.

According to Marx, only when human self-consciousness has developed to the point where the good of the individual coincides with the common good will true community be realized. As long as our interests diverge, it will be necessary to restrict liberty for the sake of equality and to restrict equality for the sake of liberty. Such restrictions will thwart the development of human powers and limit the possibility of happiness.

Marx condemned a state of simple commodity production because it rests on the assumption that human beings lack a common interest. For Marx, the real movement of society toward communism is at the same time a movement toward the realization of our common identity. Rather than ignoring the need for self-identity, the realization of that identity was a critical goal for him.

This analysis of the self as a species being suggests that if we need a connection to something we did not create, it would make sense to make the human species, rather than race or religion, our object of identification. Such an identification would provide a better means to foster true community and to resolve the conflicts based on race, religion, gender, class or nation.

Consequently, while Cohen was right to insist on the importance of self-identity, it is a mistake to believe that one's true identity can be defined by one's race, religion, class, gender or nationality. Such identifications, to the extent that they stand apart from, and in opposition to, other identifications, will not bring about social cooperation.

In conclusion, a careful consideration of Marx's philosophical anthropology shows that it is not one-sided in the way that Cohen has alleged. Nor can Marx's vision of communism be written off as an absurd goal unattainable by human beings. Rather, the need for human self-identity is consistent with his vision of a classless society. For Marx, only as beings conscious of ourselves as species beings, can we create a world in which the free development of each is the condition for the free development of all.

As noted in the introduction to this work, Marx's conception of the self as a species being grounds human self-identity on three common features: self-consciousness, creativity, and our social nature. These features, however, do not completely separate human beings from the rest of nature. Rather, we might distinguish ourselves from other species by our degree of creativity and self-consciousness. No matter how developed our consciousness, what unites the most intelligent being with the least intelligent is the fact that all beings are conscious subjects of experience. In the final two chapters of this work, I contend that this feature not only implies a common identity, but that it accounts for our rights and the rights of other species. Moreover, in the unity of the self lies the affirmation of life and the possibility of happiness.

Chapter 6

The Universal Self

In chapter five, we examined Marx's conception of the self as a species being. In asserting a common human identity, this conception provides a justification for social equality that is lacking in Rawls's theory of justice as fairness. Such a conception, however, fails to fully account for the value we attach to individual liberty. Nor does it adequately explain our relationship to the rest of nature. There is clearly need for further inquiry.

In exploring this matter, we should distinguish the self from the person or ego. Persons are identified by their unique characteristics and experiences. The self, on the other hand, is the subject of consciousness. What is constitutive of the self are those features common to all subjects of consciousness.

Logically, there are four ways in which the self might be characterized: One, the self does not exist; two, the self exists as a non-physical substance; three, the self exists as a physical substance; and four, the self exists, but is neither a physical nor a non-physical substance.

Of these four possibilities, the first is the least plausible. The very act of thinking about the self presupposes the existence of a self that thinks. Descartes reached this conclusion when he proclaimed *Ergo cogito sum* or "I think, therefore I am".

Following this pronouncement, Descartes characterized the self as a non-physical thinking substance, separate and distinct from the body. While his belief in the immortality of the soul made this characterization necessary, it raised more questions than it answered. For example, if the self is a non-physical substance, how does it interact with physical substances? Moreover, how is it possible to distinguish between individual substances or to account for their commonality? In the end, Descartes appealed to the idea of a good and all-powerful God to ensure both the reliability of our senses and to mediate our relation to others.

The unsatisfactoriness of Cartesian dualism engendered the third characterization of the self, that of a physical substance. The doctrine of physicalism identifies the self with the body, making mental events dependent upon physical events. While neuropsychology has demonstrated some correspondence between brain states and mental events, it is doubtful that a purely empirical psychology can adequately explain the self because there is a qualitative difference between matter and consciousness.

This qualitative difference makes it unlikely that neuropsychology will develop a convincing explanation for such non-physical phenomena as will, reason, instinct, creativity, imagination, conscience, and the actual value we place on morality, truth, beauty, equality and liberty. Furthermore, the design and lawfulness of nature suggest the existence of an intelligence inherent in the universe. In rejecting the existence of any fundamental intelligence, physicalism would appear to rule out a common identity or interest that might provide the key to human happiness.

Moreover, if the self is nothing more than the product of physical forces, how can we account for the apparent constancy of the self; for the fact that we believe that we are the same being from moment to moment? The philosopher David Hume grappled with this question without success. For Hume, the concept of self-identity requires something invariable and uninterrupted. Hume believed that we form an idea of self-identity by discovering and producing resemblances and causal relations. But he also noted that because our ideas and impressions change, our idea of self-identity must be fictitious.[1]

Hume drew this conclusion from the following principles: 1) Distinct perceptions are distinct existences; and 2) The mind never perceives any real connection among distinct existences. Hume claimed that these two principles are inconsistent.[2] Since they are not inconsistent with each other, commentators have questioned what Hume might have meant by this statement.

Daniel Flage has written that Hume believed that there would be no problem with the idea of self-identity if our perceptions inhered in something simple and individual or if the mind could perceive some real connection between perceptions.[3] Hume's two principles, however, are inconsistent with the belief in the simplicity of the mind.

In rejecting the Cartesian doctrine of substance, according to Flage, Hume was forced to ascribe metaphysical independence to our perceptions. But if perceptions are independent, then the mind cannot be simple and enduring through time. If, as Hume assumed, all ideas are copies of sense impressions, and if belief is nothing more than a lively idea, then it is impossible to believe in the simplicity of the mind. However, we do, in fact, so believe.

Hume could not explain our belief in identity of the self because no idea can adequately describe the self, a conclusion which again suggests the inadequacy of a purely empirical psychology. These difficulties for a physicalist conception point to the final conception of the self, described by the Buddhist doctrine of no-mind.

This doctrine may be said to distinguish the Eastern conception of the self as the subject of consciousness from Western conceptions of substance.[4] On this view, there is only one self which creates the universe and animates every living being.

This universal self is neither physical nor substantial. This characterization of the self avoids the pitfalls of Cartesian dualism without collapsing the self into the body. Because the self is the subject, rather than the object, of consciousness, it cannot be located in space and time. Because it is embodied, however, we experience reality within space and time.

The Eastern conception of the self as neither physical nor substantial is consistent with the teachings of Western idealism and phenomenology. Hegel, for example, offered a similar description of the self when he wrote:

> Reason is spirit, when its certainty of being all reality has been raised to the level of truth, and reason is consciously aware of itself as its own world, and of the world as itself....When reason 'observes' this pure unity of ego and existence, the unity of subjectivity and objectivity, of for-itself-ness and in-it-selfness this unity is immanent, has the character of implicitness or of being; and consciousness of reason finds itself."[5]

Likewise, the philosopher Edmund Husserl observed that consciousness is always consciousness of something. Pure consciousness can never be an object for itself. Following Kant and Hegel, Husserl used the term "transcendental ego" in the following passage to describe a single consciousness shared by all subjects:

> [M]y own phenomenologically self-contained essence can be posited in an absolute sense, as I am the Ego who invests the being of the world...with existential validity, as an existence (Sein) which wins for me from my own life's pure essence meaning and substantiated validity. I myself as this individual essence, posited absolutely, as the open infinite field of pure phenomenological data and their inseparable unity, am the 'transcendental Ego'; the absolute positing means that the world is no longer 'given' to me in advance, its validity of a simple existent, but that henceforth it is exclusively my Ego that is given...purely as that which has being in itself.[6]

The abstract language of Hegel and Husserl might clarified by asking if there are any characteristics of consciousness that differentiate the consciousness of one subject from that of another? Because consciousness cannot take itself for an object, it would appear that there can be no difference between one subject of consciousness as subject and any other subject of consciousness.

This observation represents the converse of Gottfried Leibnitz's principle of the identity of indiscernibles. Leibnitz held that no two objects can be identical in all respects, but differ in number. If two objects are indiscernible, they must be identical.[7] Because one subject of consciousness as subject is indiscernible from any other subject, there can be only one subject of consciousness.

Stated differently, we can identity individuals by reference to objects of consciousness—bodies, perceptions, thoughts and feelings—but never by reference to consciousness itself. While the objects of consciousness can be differentiated, the subject remains the same. It is this undifferentiated subject of consciousness that constitutes the universal self.

The conception of a universal self is consistent with the revelations of modern physics. For example, in *The Tao of Physics,* physicist Fritjof Capra explained that the discoveries of quantum physics and relativity theory have demolished the classical concepts of solid objects and strictly deterministic laws of nature, revealing a basic oneness of the universe.[8] Capra wrote:

> As we penetrate into matter, nature…appears as a complicated web of relations between the various parts of the whole. These relations always include the observer in an essential way. The human observer constitutes the final link in the chain of observational processes, and the properties of any atomic object can only be understood in terms of the objects interaction with the observer. This means that the classical ideal of an objective description of nature is no longer valid. The Cartesian partition between the I and the world, between the observer and the observed, cannot be made when dealing with atomic matter. In atomic physics, we can never speak about nature without, at the same time, speaking about ourselves.[9]

In contrast to the Cartesian partition between the I and the world, Capra noted that the teachings of Buddha and other Eastern mystics present a world view that is consistent with that of modern physics. The mystics, according to Capra, see all things and events as different aspects of the same ultimate reality. The highest aim of the mystics "is to become aware of this unity and mutual interrelation of all things, to transcend the notion of an isolated individual self and to identify themselves with the ultimate reality."[10]

In *The Tao of Physics*, Capra described what physicist Geoffrey Chew has called the "bootstrap hypothesis," a theory in which the universe is seen as a dynamic web of interrelated events. On this view, there are no fundamental properties and the overall consistency of their interrelationships determines the structure of the universe. According to Chew: "[T]he bootstrap conjecture implies that the existence of consciousness, along with all other aspects of nature, is necessary for self-consistency of the whole."[11]

Capra further noted that:

> This view... is in perfect harmony with the views of the Eastern mystical traditions....
> In the Eastern view, human beings, like all other life forms, are parts of an inseparable organic whole. Their intelligence, therefore, implies that the whole, too, is intelligent. Man is seen as the living proof of cosmic intelligence; in us, the universe repeats over and over again its ability to produce forms through which it becomes consciously aware of itself. [12]

Capra found the Buddhist world view to be compatible with the insights of a modern physics that have shattered the classical notions of an absolute time and space, elementary solid particles, a strictly causal nature of physical phenomena, and the ideal of an objective description of nature.[13]

According to Capra, relativity theory has shown us that two events which are seen as occurring simultaneously by one observer may occur in different sequences for others. Moreover, experiments have confirmed that as velocities approach the speed of light objects become shorter and clocks run slower.[14]

Relativity theory has also demonstrated that three dimensional space is curved by the gravity of massive bodies. It is the curvature of space around black holes that prevents light from escaping. Capra also noted that the curvature of space affects the flow of time, when he wrote that: "To an outside observer, the flow of time on the star's surface slows down as the star collapses and it stops altogether at the event horizon. Therefore, the complete collapse of the star takes an infinite time."[15]

The paradoxical nature of relativity theory is also reflected in the discoveries of quantum physics. The physicist Nihls Bohr coined the term "complementarity" to describe the fact that light may be described both as a wave and as a particle. Werner Heisenberg's uncertainty principle further demonstrated that we cannot simultaneously measure a particle's position and momentum. As a consequence, our knowledge of atomic processes is based entirely on probabilities.

Capra has pointed out that Einstein was unwilling to accept Bohr's interpretation of quantum theory as inherently indeterministic, an opinion he expressed in his famous statement that God does not play dice with the universe. In an attempt to demonstrate the existence of local hidden variables that could explain the experimental findings of quantum physics, Einstein devised a thought experiment that has come to be known as the Einstein-Podolsky-Rosen (EPR) experiment. According to Einstein, Bohr's interpretation of quantum theory should allow an experimenter to place a particle in a measuring device at one location and, in doing so, instantly influence another particle arbitrarily far away. Because relativity theory has demonstrated that no signal can travel faster than light, Einstein believed that Bohr's interpretation proved that quantum theory is incomplete

However, Capra pointed out that the physicist John Bell has derived a theorem proving that the existence of local hidden variables is inconsistent with the statistical predictions of quantum theory. According to Capra:

> The experiment involves two electrons spinning in opposite directions, so that their total spin is zero.... as they go off in opposite directions, their combined spin will still be zero, and once they are separated by a large distance, their individual spins are measured....

> Suppose now that the spin of particle 1 is measured along a vertical axis and is found to be 'up'. Because the combined spin of the two particles is zero, this measurement tells us that the spin of particle 2 must be 'down'. Thus, by measuring the spin of particle 1 we obtain an indirect measurement of particle 2 without in any way disturbing that particle.... The crucial point is that we can choose our axis of measurement at the last minute, when the electrons are already far apart. At the instant we perform our measurement on particle 1, particle 2, which may be thousands of miles away, will acquire a definite spin along the chosen axis. How does particle 2 know which axis we have chosen? There is no time for it to receive that information by any conventional signal....

> According to Einstein, since no signal can travel faster then the speed of light, it is impossible that the measurement performed on one electron will instantly determine the direction of the other electron's spin, thousands of miles away. According to Bohr, the two-particle system is an indivisible whole, even if the particles are separated by a great distance.... Bell's theorem supports Bohr's position and proves rigorously that Einstein's view of physical reality as consisting of independent, spatially separated elements is incompatible with the laws of quantum theory. In other words, Bell's theorem demonstrates that the universe is fundamentally interconnected, interdependent, and inseparable.[16]

As noted above, the revelations of relativity and quantum theory have fundamentally altered our conception of an absolute time and space and a strictly causal nature of physical phenomena. Instead, modern physics teaches us that the universe is interconnected, interdependent, and inseparable.

According to Capra, this fundamental unity of nature is further confirmed by the fact that all particles of a given kind are identical in that they have the same mass, electric charge and other characteristic properties.[17]

Noting that mass is not a measure of substance, but a form of energy; that all particles can be transmuted into other particles; and that particles can be created from energy and vanish into energy,.[18] Capra wrote that:

> The creation and destruction of material particles is one of the most impressive consequences of the equivalence of mass and energy. In the collision process of high energy physics, mass is no longer conserved. The colliding particles can be destroyed and their masses may be transformed partly into the masses and partly into the kinetic energies of the newly created particles. Only the total energy involved in such a process…is conserved. . . .

> The discovery that mass is nothing but a form of energy has forced us to modify our concept of a particle in an essential way. In modern physics, mass is no longer associated with a material substance, and hence particles are not seen as consisting of any basic 'stuff', but as bundles of energy. Since energy is associated with activity, with processes, the implication is that the nature of subatomic particles is intrinsically dynamic.[19]

Capra went on to point out that the conception of a dynamic universe is consistent with the teachings of Eastern mysticism when he wrote that:

> The distinction between matter and empty space finally had to be abandoned when it became evident that virtual particles can come into being simultaneously out of the void, and vanish again into the void, without any nucleon or other strongly interacting particle being present.…Here then, is the closest parallel to the Void of Eastern mysticism in modern physics. Like the Eastern Void, the 'physical vacuum'—as it is called in field theory—is not a state of mere nothingness, but contains the potentiality for all forms of the particle world. These forms, in turn, are not independent physical entities but merely transparent manifestations of the underlying Void.[20]

The fact that matter may by created out of nothing is of profound importance to our understanding of the origin of the universe and of the role of its creator. Creation *ex nihilo* suggests the existence of a non-physical intelligence that accounts for both consciousness and the lawfulness of nature. The pursuit of this creator provided the motivation for Deepak Chopra's insightful book, *How to Know God.*[21]

According to Chopra, ultimate reality is called Brahman in Hinduism,

Dharmkaya in Buddhism, and Tao in Taoism. He noted that there is a recurring theme in Hindu mythology that God becomes the world which then becomes God. In the process, an individual may overcome suffering and obtain enlightenment.

According to the Hinduism, suffering is caused by ignorance about the nature of reality; identification with the ego; attraction toward objects of desire; repulsion from objects of desire; and the fear of death.[22] According to Chopra: "When a person forgets he has a soul, that his source is rooted in eternal Being, separation results, and from separation all other pain and suffering follows."[23]

Like Capra, Chopra has pointed to the parallels between Eastern mysticism and modern physics. Both world views emphasize the impermanence of the observed world and interrelatedness of all things, including the subjects of consciousness. Chopra, a physician, has claimed that the pursuit of God represents the highest instinct to know ourselves. In his work, he described seven stages of God which correspond to seven brain states, ranging from the fight or flight response to the sacred response. He also offered practical suggestions to guide us in our pursuit of the sacred.

Chopra's conception of God as the source of existence is informed by religion, neuroscience and quantum physics. In his book, he described the universe as a projection of God's nature as an inherent organizing intelligence. He also observed that motion is an intrinsic property of matter; that matter and energy are interchangeable; and that consciousness is an inseparable part of the material world.

In an effort to demonstrate the consistency between Big Bang theory and the views of Eastern mysticism, Chopra wrote:

> The best working theory about creation reads as follows: Before the Big Bang, space was unbounded, expanded like an accordion into infinite pleats or dimensions, while time existed in seed form, an eternal presence without events and therefor needing no past, present, or future. This state was utterly void in one sense and utterly full in another. It contained nothing we could possibly perceive, yet the potential for everything resided here. As the Vedic seers declared, neither existence nor non-existence could be found, since those terms apply only to things that have a beginning, middle, and end. Physicists often refer to this state as a *singularity*: space, time, and the entire material universe were once contained in a point. A singularity is conceived as the smallest dot you can imagine, and therefore not a dot at all.
>
> Now if you can imagine that the cosmos exploded into being in a dazzling flash of light from this one point, you must then go a step further. *Because the pre-creation state has*

no time, it is still here. The Big Bang has never happened in the virtual domain, and yet paradoxically all Big Bangs have happened—no matter how many times the universe expands across billions of light-years, only to collapse back onto itself and withdraw back into the void, nothing will change at the virtual level. This is as close as physics has come to the religious notion of a God who is omnipresent, omniscient, and omnipotent. *Omni* means all, and the virtual state, since it has no boundaries of any kind, is properly called the All.[24]

According to Chopra, Big Bang theory, general and special relativity, and quantum theory all demonstrate that subject and object, matter and energy, and time and space are all forms of the same Being. He further elaborated as follows:

Throughout the universe, the photon is the most basic unit of electromagnetic energy. Every single thing you can perceive is actually a swirling cloud of energy. At the moment of the Big Bang the universe exploded with energy that now forms everything in existence, and buried somewhere under the skin of every object or event, the primordial light still burns. Being the essence of transformation, primordial light isn't always the same shape or form billions of years later. A granite cliff is solid, hard, flintlike light; an impulse of love is sweet, emotional light; the firing of a neuron is an instant flash of invisible light. Yet as dissimilar as they appear, when broken down to their most basic components, all things derive from the same primal stuff.[25]

In his book, Chopra equated spirit with the virtual domain; mind with the quantum domain; and the visible universe with material reality. This tripartite division offers a striking parallel to the descriptions of the self offered by Plato and Freud. Chopra also maintained that the worship of God is worship of the self and that the same "I" that gives a person a sense of identity extends "beyond the physical body, expanding to embrace nature, the universe, and ultimately pure spirit."[26]

Chopra also declared that:

The most mystical of the gospels is the Book of John. Consider its description of creation: "In the beginning was the word, and the word was with God, and the word was God." In other parts of the Bible, a writer who wanted to refer to divine wisdom would call it "the word," but here John says "the word *is* God." Clearly no ordinary word is implied. Something like the following is meant: Before there was time and space, a faint vibration existed outside the cosmos. This vibration had everything contained in it—all universes, all events, all time and space. This primordial vibration was with God. As far as we can fathom, it *is* God. Divine intelligence was compressed in this "word," and when the time came for the universe to be born, the "word" transformed itself into energy and matter.[27]

In this passage, Chopra clearly made the attempt to reconcile the insights of science and religion in a manner the preserves the essential message of both disciplines. Turning his attention to human consciousness, he addressed the work of Wilder Penfield, a brain researcher who posed the following question: "Where in the brain can you find any mechanism that possesses intuition, creativity, insight, imagination, understanding, intent, knowing, will, decision, or spirit? Indeed all the higher functions of the brain still cannot create the qualities that make us most human."[28]

In response to this question, Chopra noted that neuroscience has been unable to explain how the mind survives traumas or how we generate new thoughts or insights.[29] He also noted that neuroscience has demonstrated that individual cells display memory, recognition, identity and self-preservation along with a willingness to die to protect the body from infection.[30] Finally, he observed that the DNA within each cell contains an intelligent code that governs cell development in a way that makes life possible.[31] According to Chopra, our DNA is aware of the proper time to act in the interest of the individual and the species.[32]

The presence of an organizing intelligence as a constitutive feature of existence finds support in the observations of Stephen Hawking. In *A Brief History of Time,* Hawking described the origin of the universe in accordance with the Big Bang theory of creation. Because galaxies are moving apart at increasing speed, Big Bang theory postulates that at the beginning of the universe the space between galaxies was zero. According to Hawking, at the time of the Big Bang "the density of the universe and the curvature of space-time would have been infinite.... Such a point is an example of what mathematicians call a singularity."[33]

The idea that the entire universe, including the consciousness necessary to comprehend the universe, has emerged from a singularity strongly suggests that consciousness is an essential feature of the universe, rather than a fortuitous development. In an analysis that has been cited in support of the idea of a universal intelligence, Hawking stated that the laws of science:

> contain many fundamental numbers, like the size of the electric charge of the electron and the ratio of the masses of the proton and the electron.... The remarkable fact is that the values of these numbers seem to have been very finely adjusted to make possible the development of life. For example, if the electric charge of the electron had been

only slightly different, stars either would have been unable to burn hydrogen and helium, or else they would not have exploded.... [I]t seems clear that there are relatively few ranges of values for the numbers that would allow the development of any form of intelligent life. Most sets of values would give rise to universes that, although they might be very beautiful, would contain no one able to wonder at that beauty.[34]

Hawking has also noted that "[i]f the rate of expansion one second after the big bang had been smaller by even one part in a hundred thousand million million, the universe would have recollapsed before it ever reached its present size."[35]

The insights of Capra, Chopra and Hawking are of profound importance. Each bears witness to a view of reality in which the entire universe, including the minds necessary to comprehend the universe, has emerged from a single point of infinite density. This fundamental reality—whether we call it God, the All, the Void or a singularity—is our common identity and our ultimate goal. In understanding this truth about the self lies the possibility of happiness.

As noted before, this conception of a universal self is not a new idea. In addition to the teachings of Eastern mysticism, Nietzsche alluded to it when he wrote that in the Dionysian dithyramb the veil of *maya* is annihilated and our oneness with nature is revealed. Likewise, Freud believed that prior to the development of the ego, the infant experiences a feeling of oneness with the world that he described as "oceanic." Marcuse speculated the that taboo on incest was a response to the threat posed by the instinctual desire to return to this original unity.

The conception of a universal self is also implicit in the teachings of many religions. For example, the promise of eternal life is a central tenet of Taoism, Buddhism, Hinduism, Islam, Judaism and Christianity. The idea of a common identity is also consistent with Christ's assertion that whatever you do to the least of my brethren, you do unto me. Moreover, this conception supports the admonition that we should do unto others as we would have them do unto us. This "golden rule" of Christianity found its philosophical expression in Kant's categorical imperative.

The conception of a universal self is also consistent with reports of mystical experience throughout history. One commentator has summarized such reports as follows:

Those who have had the more profound type of mystical experiences, no matter in what age or to what race or creed they have belonged, tell us the same fundamental things: The sense of separateness vanished in an all-embracing unity, there is a certain knowledge of immortality, there is an enormously enhanced appreciation of values, and there is knowledge that at the heart of the universe is Joy and Beauty.

Those who have known such an experience are always profoundly impressed by its significance as a revelation of truth. There is from then onwards, not the satisfaction of an intellectual answer to life's ultimate questions, but a serenity born of the knowledge that all is well, and that the secret purpose of the universe is good beyond all telling.[36]

This feeling of unity also reveals itself in the beautiful illusion of artistic expression and in the experience of the erotic. In moments of ecstasy, our consciousness of separateness and of the passage of time is suspended. A similar experience may result from meditation or the use of psychotropic drugs. In each instance, the partition between the I and the world is abolished, revealing an underlying unity.

The existence of a universal self may also account for the presence of conscience. We experience guilt and remorse when causing harm to others because we know that every harm is a harm to the self. This truth provides the moral foundation for a criminal law that punishes persons who wilfully harm others without excuse or justification.

The existence of a universal self may also explain the direction of history from slavery toward freedom. Although this movement has been uneven, the progressive role of liberalism and the appeal of a classless society testify to the importance of our interest in liberty and equality. As our collective understanding grows, this interest will demand new social institutions and arrangements. On this view, social justice is a developmental project. The achievement of a perfect liberty and a perfect equality is an ideal to which some societies are closer than others.

The conception of a universal self also accords with our praise of altruism and our rejection of egoism, especially those expressions which degrade others for the sake of self-aggrandizement. Some critics of liberalism have proposed to replace individualism with altruism as the guiding principle of our jurisprudence.[37] The value of altruism is apparent if the self is universal, but far from evident from the perspective of mutually disinterested individuals.[38]

A common identity also comports with the Platonic desire for the everlasting possession of the good. On this account, truth, goodness and beauty are constitutive of the self. In addition to the form of the good, however, Plato introduced the idea of the divided self. The tripartite division of the soul into rational, emotional and appetitive elements provided the framework for the noble lie; the claim that persons should be assigned to social roles on the basis of their fixed natures. For Plato, the lie was justified by the need to preserve a social order based on human slavery. However, the continuation of an order of servitude and domination has become irrational in a culture of affluence.

Finally, the unity of the self is consistent with the hypothesis of a death instinct in which a divided self seeks to restore an original unity. In addition to the accounts offered by Nietzsche, Freud, Marcuse and Adorno, a depiction of the death instinct is found in Jean Paul Sartre's novel, *Nausea*. As Sartre's protagonist Roquentin ponders his existence in a park, he comes to realize that the nausea he has been experiencing "is no longer an illness or a passing fit: it is I."[39]

Like Nietzsche before him, Sartre invoked the imagery of the veil when he wrote:

> Existence had suddenly unveiled itself. It had lost the harmless look of an abstract category: it was the very paste of things...the diversity of things, their individuality, were only an appearance, a veneer....

> Everything is born without reason, prolongs itself out of weakness and dies by chance.... I knew it was the World, the naked World suddenly revealing itself, and I choked with rage at this gross, absurd being....There had been nothing before it. Nothing. There had never been a moment in which it could not have existed. That was what worried me: of course there was no reason for this flowing larva to exist. But it was impossible for it not to exist.... I shouted 'filth! what rotten filth!' and shook myself to get rid of this sticky filth, but it held fast and there was so much, tons and tons of existence, endless: I stifled at the depths of this immense weariness.[40]

Sartre's experience of nausea, however, did not end with these observations. As Roquentin walked to the gate, he turned to look back at the park. At that moment, "the garden smiled at me. I leaned against the gate and watched a long time. The smile of the trees, of the laurel, meant something; that was the real secret of existence.... I could not understand it, even if I could have stayed leaning against the gate for a century."[41]

In these passages, there is a fascinating juxtaposition of nausea at the fullness of existence with the smile of the trees. This juxtaposition represents the conflict of the life and death instincts. Roquentin's experience of nausea sprang from his realization that there is no end to existence. Since existence entails suffering, happiness is impossible.

However, the smile of the trees reveals the secret of existence. While Sartre claimed not to understand this secret, the smile reveals the presence of a joy that can overcome suffering and the spell of the death instinct. The smile accords with Nietzsche's claim that: "All joy loves eternity." It attests to the triumph of life over death; good over evil; happiness over despair.

From the perspective of a universal self, the death instinct may be seen as the attempt to restore a divided self to an original state of unity; to reverse our individuation. The death instinct may also explain sadomasochism and the weakness of will displayed when we perform acts we know to be contrary to our self-interest.

In sum, the hypothesis of a death instinct seeking to restore an original unity may explain the order of domination and servitude, the division of labor and the desire for instinctual gratification. It may account for both the allure of the erotic and the bonds of community. In the universality of the self is the realization of the Platonic guest for permanence.

Finally, we must consider the question of evil. For Plato, evil was the result of ignorance. One who knows the good, will do it. While this may be true, it begs the question of why we are ignorant. Why would a universal self create a world of pain, ugliness and injustice if it could have used its knowledge to create a world of joy, beauty and justice? In other words, why are we not already happy?

Conventional wisdom blames our unhappiness on a variety of factors ranging from original sin and moral weakness to economic scarcity and social inequality. However, the answer to this question necessarily involves a paradox because division lies at heart of existence.

In creating an entire universe out of nothing, the self must play every role. It is both subject and object, mind and body, creator and creature, the one and the many. The opposites of life and death, truth and falsehood, good and evil, beauty and ugliness, and pleasure and pain reflect this fundamental duality. Because no quality can exist without its opposite, pain is the prelude to pleasure just as ignorance is the preclude to knowledge. For that reason, while it is true that suffering is the result of ignorance, it is an ignorance borne of necessity and endured for the sake of what is to come.

The joy of what is to come was eloquently expressed in Walt Whitman's famous poem "Song of Myself." In it he wrote:

The clock indicates the moment—but what does eternity indicate?
We have thus far exhausted trillions of winters and summers,
There are trillions ahead, and trillions ahead of them.
Births have brought us richness and variety.
And other births will bring us richness and variety....
And I say to mankind, Be not curious about God,
For I who am curious about each am not curious about God,
(No array of terms can say how much I am at peace about God and about death.)
I hear and behold God in every object, yet understand God not in the least....
And as to you Death, and you bitter hug of mortality, it is idle to try to alarm me....
And as to you Life I reckon you are the leavings of many deaths,
(No doubt I have died myself ten thousand times before.)...
There is that in me—I do not know what it is—but I know it is in me....
It is not chaos or death—it is form, union, plan—it is eternal life—it is Happiness.[42]

The self that has created the universe is the same self that will recreate the universe based on the power of its reason and its knowledge of the good. With this knowledge, we can transform our social practices and institutions for the sake of human happiness. It is to this task of social transformation that we must turn our attention.

Chapter 7

The Just Society

In chapter one, we discussed the perennial concern of philosophy with the pursuit of happiness. We also explored the thesis of a divided self in search of an original unity. In chapter two, we discussed the existence of a death instinct which, along with the development of technological rationality and a capitalist division of labor, stands in the way of a general happiness.

In chapters three and four, we examined the conflict over the priority of the right or the good in deontological and teleological theories of justice. We also noted that John Rawls's theory of justice as fairness does not give priority to the right over the good, but it does give priority to liberty over equality. The priority of liberty is the necessary result of a conception of the self as an autonomous chooser of ends.

In chapters five and six, we considered a conception of the self as both a species being and as a universal being that is the source of all creation. While the self may be universal, it manifests itself in the world as subject and object, mind and body, creator and creature, the one and the many.

In this chapter, I contend that it is precisely because of our duality that liberty and equality are of fundamental importance. I also contend that any institutional arrangement which promotes one of these values at the expense of the other will fail to produce social justice or human happiness.

As noted throughout this work, the dispute over the priority of liberty or equality turns on competing conceptions of the self. Individual liberty is fundamental for those who conceive the self to be an autonomous creator of value. Social equality is fundamental for those who conceive the self to be the product of social discovery. Moreover, equality is fundamental because the value of our lives is largely determined by the way we are regarded by others.

However, a complete description of the self—and compelling principles of justice—must involve both creation and discovery, liberty and equality. What is discovered is our common identity. What is created is the meaning and purpose of our lives. Somewhat paradoxically, discovery entails an individual act of reflection; creation a social act of interpretation. The discovery of our identity as the creator of value confirms the importance of liberty, while the creation of meaning and purpose confirms the importance of equality.

The importance of liberty is also confirmed by the fact that for a universal being there can be no measure of value external to the self. As Nietzsche and others have remarked, man is the creator of value. If so, then the liberty to pursue our own conception of the good life is essential for human flourishing. As the creator of value, we must reserve the right to alter our traditions and to reject the demands of society when they become unreasonable.

The importance of equality is further confirmed by the fact that we cannot fully respect ourselves if we are not respected by others. For that reason, a just society must respect the equality of all persons as moral agents subject to the rule of law.

It is precisely because the self is both the creator of value and the product of social discovery that individual liberty and social equality are of fundamental importance to the pursuit of happiness. To further this pursuit, it will be necessary to establish and preserve social institutions and practices which promote both liberty and equality, without favoring one at the expense of the other.

The task of achieving a balance between the goals of individual liberty and social equality is reflected in the design of the basic institutions of most constitutional democracies. For example, a federal constitution limits the powers of the central government by reserving certain powers to the states and to the people and by identifying basic rights that are guaranteed to every citizen. A constitution may also limit the power of particular branches of government by creating a system of checks and balances between them.

Constitutional democracies demonstrate a commitment to individual liberty by guaranteeing such rights as freedom of speech and association, freedom of the press, freedom of religion, freedom of movement and occupation, the right to bodily integrity, the right to marry, the right of privacy and the right to own property. A commitment to individual liberty is also reflected in a criminal law that limits liberty only when necessary to prevent harm to others. The harm principle also governs tort law where liability is imposed for harm caused by wilfulness, recklessness or negligence.

Constitutional democracies demonstrate a commitment to social equality by guaranteeing, in addition to an equal set of civil liberties, the right to vote and to hold office. Citizens are also granted the right to due process and to the equal protection of the laws. Due process requires notice and an opportunity to be heard before an individual right may be abridged by governmental action. Equal protection means that like cases must be treated alike and that fundamental rights may not be abridged without a compelling state interest. Equality before the law is also reflected in statutes prohibiting discrimination and requiring equal opportunity. Furthermore, the principle of promise keeping embodied in contract law reflects a commitment to both liberty and equality because only as free and equal citizens can we bind each other to the terms of our agreements.

Because we cannot fully respect ourselves if we do not enjoy the same rights and liberties that are enjoyed by other citizens, an authoritarian regime will be unjust no matter how egalitarian its system of distribution. In such states, true equality is impossible because the rulers enjoy liberties not enjoyed by the ruled. In response to the task described by Rousseau, we can say that the achievement of true equality will require the liberty with which to choose equality as a fundamental value. Until we achieve a true liberty and a true equality, the recognition of individual rights and the rule of law will be necessary to preserve the social order.[1]

While constitutional democracies demonstrate, to various degrees, a commitment to both individual liberty and social equality, a capitalist division of labor has alienated us from the product of our labor and from our solidarity with other human beings. While capitalism has increased the material wealth of society, it has also created a permanent underclass of individuals who cannot satisfy their material, social or spiritual needs.

The abolition of capitalism raises an important question for any theory of justice. Would the abolition of the capitalist division of labor violate the fundamental right of persons to own property? While the abolition of capitalism need not deny individuals the right to own personal property, it would deny them the right to own the means of production and to control the labor of others.

By way of analogy, the rights of a capitalist may be compared with those of a slaveholder. Both own the means of production and both control the labor of others. In a slave system, the liberty of the slaveholder is in conflict with the liberty and equality of the slave. In the same manner, but to a lesser degree in a capitalist system, the liberty of the capitalist is in conflict with the liberty and equality of the worker.

All would agree that slavery is unjust because the slaveholder's exercise of liberty precludes both the slave's exercise of liberty and his entitlement to the respect accorded to equals. In other words, a slave system is clearly incompatible with a social order designed to maximize the liberty and equality of all persons.

Likewise, a capitalist economic system limits the liberty and equality of workers by denying them control of their labor, which is their life activity as the creators of value. This diminution of liberty also results in the loss of equality as workers enjoy fewer rights and privileges than do capitalists. As a result, class divisions limit our opportunities for social cooperation and our ability to reach consensus on the common good. These divisions find expression in our politics, our law, and our other social practices and institutions.

Disparities in the legal rights and obligations accorded to the members of distinct economic classes limit the ability of our legal system to promote the common good, while imbalances in power and wealth influence both the nature of our substantive rights and the manner in which those rights are exercised. While our legal system mediates conflicts between such groups as employers and employees, producers and consumers, and landlords and tenants, it has not altered the disparities in their respective rights and obligations. Moreover, economic inequality has created social and political inequality by limiting meaningful participation in the political process and making it difficult for the poor to exercise their legal rights.

Some of the social ills created by a capitalist division of labor have been ameliorated by progressive taxation, income redistribution, public education, economic and environmental regulation, and the provision of basic public services. These efforts, however, have not produced an order of abundance. Nor have they maximized individual liberty or social equality.

As noted above, the radical objection to the capitalist division of labor is premised not on the desire for more wealth or greater efficiency, but on the satisfaction of our need for self-respect that requires treatment as an equal. As long as some individuals have the right to control the productive life of others, this need will go unsatisfied. Because the liberty of some is made possible by the servitude of others, a capitalist division of labor is inconsistent with a serious commitment to social justice or human happiness.

An economic order which accords equal respect to all persons will require democratic decision-making geared to the satisfaction of human needs. Without question, such a development will require a major redirection of public investment from the military to the civilian sector of the economy. It will also require a public policy of full employment, a living wage, universal education and health care, environmental protection, and worker health and safety.

Moreover, the achievement of social justice will require the recognition of a right to livelihood. Such a right would extend to all persons the means necessary to satisfy the need for food and clothing, housing and utilities, and education, employment and health care.

In addition, democratic decision-making through public and private institutions and associations should promote the common good by protecting us from harm and by providing goods and services needed to satisfy human needs. In return for the right to livelihood, individuals must obey the law, respect the rights of others, and participate in economic, social and cultural activities that enhance our quality of life.

Of course, a right to livelihood will have meaning only if sufficient resources exist to guarantee its exercise. There would be little value in a right to employment, for example, in a society that does not possess the means to provide jobs for its citizens. However, even in an impoverished society, a right to livelihood can serve as an organizing principle by which the distribution of benefits and burdens is decided.

A right to livelihood would establish a social minimum, but not an equal distribution of social goods, because individual needs vary and a completely equal distribution of wealth would unreasonably infringe on individual liberty. Moreover, a capitalist division of labor should be replaced, not by state socialism, but by cooperatively owned enterprises managed by their employees and subject to public regulation.

The prerequisites to human happiness—material abundance, self-knowledge and social justice—can now be seen in a new light. Technical progress has made possible an order of abundance necessary to satisfy our material needs. However, technological rationality and a capitalist division of labor have bolstered an order of domination and servitude that has repressed the possibility of human happiness. Any challenge to that order based on the priority of liberty over equality (capitalism) or on the priority of equality over liberty (socialism) will fail because, as universal beings, our happiness requires the realization of both liberty and equality.

These philosophical observations are consistent with the empirical findings of the economist Richard Layard who, in a recent study of human happiness, has shown that the dramatic increases in personal income over the past 50 years have not made us any happier.[2] In his study, Layard noted that there are seven factors that have repeatedly determined the perception of individual happiness: family relationships, financial situation, work, community and friends, health, personal freedom and personal values.[3] In order to promote the greatest possible happiness, he has called for measures to increase social equality, reduce crime, improve mental health and family stability, tax addictions, limit advertising, and enhance the moral education of children.[4] Each of these suggestions is consistent with both the social preconditions discussed by Marcuse and with the right to livelihood described above.

However, the articulation of these policy recommendations does not end our inquiry. The conception of a universal self as the subject of consciousness has important implications for our relationship with non-human species. If all sentient beings share a common consciousness, then the concept of rights is not an exclusively human consideration.

The philosopher Michael Tooley has suggested that if self-consciousness provides the basis of a right to life, then it may be appropriate to extend this right to other species.[5] According to Tooley, a person can be said to possess a right to "x" only if he is capable of desiring "x". Without a conception of oneself as a continuing subject of experience, it would be impossible to desire that one's life continue. While members of other species may not see themselves as species beings, they may possess some measure of self-consciousness. Tooley has argued that if other animals have such a self-conception, it follows that "our everyday treatment of animals is morally indefensible, and that we are in fact murdering innocent persons."[6]

Peter Singer has also questioned the sharp distinction often made between human and non-human species. He cited Bentham in support of the claim that consciousness alone is the source of the right to be free from unnecessary suffering. In *Introduction to the Principles of Morals and Legislation*, Bentham wrote that:

> a full-grown horse or dog is beyond comparison a more rational, as well as a more conversable animal, than an infant of a day, or a week, or even a month old. But suppose they were otherwise, what would it avail? The question is not, Can they reason? nor Can they talk? but Can they suffer?[7]

Singer maintained that the concept of human rights ought to be extended to other species unless it is possible to define some morally relevant trait possessed by human beings, but not by other animals. He further asserted that the capacity to experience pain is itself a sufficient ground for the right to be free from its infliction. The writings of Tooley and Singer suggest that while we need not confer the same rights on the members of other species, we must be prepared to justify our treatment of them.

There is also good reason to believe that the principles of justice governing the basic institutions of a society should extend to relationships between societies. Such an extension would require nations to promote the right to liberty and equality of all persons; to respect the sovereignty of other nations; and to adhere to the obligations imposed by international law. Moreover, the recognition of a universal right to livelihood will require a significant transfer of wealth and technical expertise from more developed nations to less developed ones.

Finally, at a time when civilization itself is under attack by international terrorism, it is critical that democratic societies do not abdicate their commitment to liberty and equality under the guise of preserving national security. While terrorism is a manifestation of the death instinct, so too is the militarism and imperialism that has contributed to its development. For that reason, a purely military response will not defeat this threat to humanity.

We must come to terms with the causes of terror. As a manifestation of the death instinct, terrorism may be seen as a reaction against institutions, societies and cultures that threaten the fundamental beliefs and values of the terrorists. Without abandoning our beliefs and values, we must find a way to coexist with cultures radically different from our own.

What is needed is dialogue and diplomacy, not invasion and imperialism. Moreover, it is always a mistake for constitutional democracies to support regimes that do not respect the dignity of their citizens. In sum, measures to overcome poverty and to promote the liberty and equality of persons will do more to reduce the threat of terrorism and armed conflict than will any exercise of military force.

The promotion of social justice throughout the world will make possible the most important step of all—the affirmation of life. Class divided societies have produced an order of domination and servitude that has repressed the life instincts. This repression has occurred because of material scarcity and the lack of human understanding With the achievement of material abundance and true community, the death instinct will lose its power over us. As alienation and division subside, so too will the domination of man and the domination of nature.

The powers which restrict and deform humanity are human powers which can be confronted and transformed. The restrictions imposed by natural necessity, on the other hand, can be reduced, but never eliminated. Even if our life span could be extended indefinitely, the lack of human perfection would guarantee sorrow. Perfection, on the other hand, would halt the passage of time. It would capture in a moment the identity of subject and object, the unity of self and world as the source of life and as the guarantee of lasting happiness.

Our preoccupation with human happiness represents a perennial concern of philosophy. The original impulse of philosophy was toward the "other world" as the hope for a happiness denied by social domination. What the two-world theory failed to acknowledge, however, is that the other world cannot exist apart from this world. The other reality exists within this reality, even if it is accessible only in memory or in the beautiful illusion of the aesthetic dimension.

From Plato's Eros as the love of perfection and immortality to Marcuse's Eros as the free expression of human instincts, philosophy has pursued the idea of human happiness. This idea represents the great unfulfilled promise of civilization. It is our responsibility to continue the pursuit.

Notes

Chapter 1

1. In Book 2 of *The Republic*, Plato claimed that the just man, even under the most unfavorable conditions, will be happy while the unjust man, with the most favorable conditions, will be miserable. See *Great Dialogues of Plato*. Trans. W.H.D. Rouse. New York: Mentor Books, 1956.

2. Aristotle argued that certain external goods such as good birth, friends, children, wealth, health, beauty, strength, fame, honor, and good luck are necessary for happiness. See *Rhetoric, The Works of Aristotle*. Ed. W.D. Ross. Oxford: Clarenden Press, 1926, 1360b20-23. For a discussion of Aristotle's theory of happiness, See V.J. McGill. *The Idea of Happiness*. New York: Edward A. Praeger, 1967.

3. According to Diogenes Laertius: "Particular pleasure is desirable for its own sake, whereas happiness is not desirable for its own sake, but for the sake of particular pleasures." Diogenes Laertius. *Lives of Eminent Philosophers*. Trans. R.D. Hicks. New York: Putnam, 1925, I, p. 217 cited in Herbert Marcuse, "On Hedonism." *Negations*. Trans. Jeremy Shapiro. Boston: Beacon Press, 1968, p. 162.

4. *Ibid.*, p. 219 cited in "On Hedonism," p. 163.

5. *Ibid.* II, p. 655 cited in "On Hedonism," p. 169.

6. Herbert Marcuse. "On Hedonism," pp. 167-168. This criticism is similar to the communitarian critique of the priority of the right over the good in liberal political theory. For the cornmunitarian, individual rights are not prior to the good of the community.

7. Plato, *The Republic*. Trans. Benjamin Jowett. Buffalo: Prometheus, 1986, 514a–521b.

8. *Great Dialogues of Plato*, p. 105.

9. See Plato. *Phaedrus* 246A-247C. The tripartite division of the soul is also discussed in *The Republic*, Book IV, 435D, Book X, 6llD-6l2A, and *Timaeus*, 69C ft.

10. Marcuse. "The Concept of Essence." *Negations*, pp. 45–46.

11. Marcuse. *Eros and Civilization*, p. 104. The emphasis on knowledge distinguishes Marcuse's conception of happiness from those of hedonism and utilitarianism.

12. Marcuse. "The Concept of Essence," pp. 53-54.

13. Marcuse. "The Affirmative Character of Culture." *Negations*, pp. 120–121.

14. Karl Marx. "Thesis on Feuerbach." *Writings of the Young Marx on Philosophy and Society*. Trans. and ed. Loyd Easton and Kurt Guddatt. Garden City, New York: Doubleday and Co. 1967, p. 402.

15. Of course, this description is too simplified. In advanced industrial societies, the emergence of large numbers of managerial, technical and professional employees complicates Marx's dichotomy between the bourgeoisie and the proletariat. In addition, many workers have acquired an "ownership" interest in their firms. These developments undermine Marx's theory of immiseration. Despite these developments, however, it is also true that in many capitalist societies disparities of wealth and power are growing and the relative autonomy accorded to professional employees only serves to mask a subtler form of domination.

16. Marx described the alienation of labor in this famous passage: "What constitutes the

alienation of labor? First, that the work is external to the worker, that it is not part of his nature: and that, consequently, he does not fulfill himself in his work but denies himself, has a feeling of misery rather than well-being, does not develop freely his mental and physical energies but is physically exhausted and mentally debased. The worker, therefore, feels himself at home only during his leisure time, whereas at work he feels homeless. His work *is* not voluntary but imposed, forced labour. It is not the satisfaction of a need, but only a means for satisfying other needs. Its alien character is clearly shown by the fact that as soon as there is no physical or other compulsion it is avoided like the plague.... Finally, the external character of work for the worker is shown by the fact that it is not his own work but work for someone else, that in work he does not belong to himself but to another person." Marx. *Early Writings.* Trans. and ed. T. B. Bottomore. New York: McGraw-Hill 1964, pp.124-125.

17. Marx. *"Economic and Philosophical Manuscripts of 1844,"* p. 135 cited in "The Foundations of Historical Materialism," p. 5.
18. Marcuse. "Philosophy and Critical Theory." *Negations*, p. 142.
19. Marcuse. *Reason and Revolution.* London: Routledge and Kegan 1969, p. 314.
20. Marcuse. "The Concept of Essence," p. 72.
21. Marcuse. "Some Social Implications of Modern Technology." *The Essential Frankfurt School Reader.* Ed. Andrew Arato and Eike Gebhardt. New York: Continuum 1982, p. 131. This claim earned Marcuse enmity from some social radicals. It is consistent with the claim he advanced in *One-Dimensional Man* that individuals have been blinded by a technological veil.
22. Sigmond Freud. *Civilization and its Discontents.* Trans. and Ed. James Strachey. New York: W.W. Norton, 1962.
23. Marcuse. *Eros and Civilization.* Boston: Beacon Press, 1966, p. 235.
24. Marcuse. *The Aesthetic Dimension.* Boston: Beacon Press, 1978, p. 9.
25. Marcuse. *Eros and Civilization,* p. 231.

Chapter 2

1. Friedrich Nietzsche. *The Birth of Tragedy.* Trans. Walter Kaufmann. New York: Random House, 1967, p. 23.
2. *Ibid.*, pp. 39–40.
3. Freud. *Beyond the Pleasure Principle.* Trans. and ed. James Strachey. New York: Liveright, 1961, p. 30.
4. *Ibid.*, pp. 49–50.
5. Freud. *Civilization and Its Discontents.* Trans. and ed. James Strachey. New York: W.W. Norton and Co. 1962, p. 69.
6. Freud. *Beyond the Pleasure Principle*, p. 55.
7. *Ibid.*
8. *Ibid.*
9. Marcuse. *Eros and Civilization,* pp. 234–235.
10. Freud. *Beyond the Pleasure Principle*, p. 2.
11. Freud. *Civilization and Its Discontents*, pp.70 ff.

12. *Ibid.*, p. 15. This sense of identity with the external world parallels the Dionysian rapture described by Nietzsche.

13. Marcuse. *Eros and Civilization*, p. 76.

14. *Ibid.*, p. 136.

15. *Ibid.*, pp. 60–65.

16. *Ibid.*, p. 3.

17. *Ibid.*, pp. 44 ff.

18. *Ibid.*, pp. 16–17.

19. Marcuse. *One-Dimensional Man.* Boston: Beacon Press, 1964, p. 148.

20. Marx. *Capital*, Vol. 1. Ed. Ben Fowkes. New York: Vintage Books 1977, p. 165.

21. Marcuse. "Some Social Implications of Modern Technology," pp. 138 ff. It should be noted that Marcuse accepted technical progress as a necessary aspect of a new society. He never embraced the anti-technological outlook of the back to nature movement.

22. While matter-of-factness itself is not new, the social organization which it defines as changed considerably. Marcuse wrote that: "Matter-of-factness animated ancient materialism and hedonism, it was responsible in the struggle of modern physical science against spiritual oppression, and in the revolutionary rationalism of the Enlightenment. The new attitude differs from all these in the highly rational compliance which typifies it. The facts directing man's thought and action are not those of a nature which must be accepted in order to be mastered, or those of society which must be changed because they no longer correspond to human needs and potentialities. Rather are they those of the machine process, which itself appears the embodiment of rationality and expediency." *Ibid.*, p. 143.

23. *Ibid.* This characterization of modern society as a machine process is consistent with Marx's description of alienated labor. For Marcuse, the fetish of technical efficiency is not only applied to the labor process, it pervades the entire society. The pervasiveness of technological rationality masks the irrationality of contemporary life and blocks efforts to understand the source of our unhappiness.

24. *Ibid.*, p. 154.

25. According to Marcuse, the reign of terror in National Socialist Germany was sustained not only by brute force but also by "the ingenious manipulation of the power inherent in technology: the intensification of labor, propaganda, the training of youths and workers, the organization of the governmental, industrial and party bureaucracy...follow the lines of greatest technological efficiency." *Ibid.*, p. 139.

26. It is important to note, however, that there are significant differences between the authoritarian state represented by National Socialism in Germany and the liberal democratic state. In the latter, individual choice is largely unconstrained. Marcuse acknowledged this difference, but held that with techniques developed from psychological and marketing studies, the loyalty of the consumer is elicited in a more subtle manner. Conformity is won with the appearance of freedom. Happiness is replaced with the temporary gratification of manufactured needs.

27. Theodor Adorno. "Freudian Theory and the Pattern of Fascist Propaganda." *The Essential Frankfurt School Reader,* pp. 118–137.

28. *Ibid.*, p. 124.

29. *Ibid.*, p. 126 quoting Freud. *Group Psychology and the Analysis of the Ego.* London: The

International Psychoanalytical Press, 1922, p. 80.

30. As Freud noted: "Every religion is in this same way a religion of love for all those whom it embraces; while cruelty and intolerance towards those who do not belong to it are natural to every religion." *Ibid.*, p. 129 quoting Freud, *Ibid.*, p. 50.

31. While Marcuse's rejection of technological rationality was unwavering, his attitude toward technology itself was ambivalent. He never renounced the possibility that mechanization could shift the focus of labor away from the necessities of production to an arena of free human realization. The reduction of scarcity and the abolition of competitive pursuits could provide the basis for greater social freedom. While it could not guarantee perennial happiness, it would mean a reduction in the alienation of labor, freedom from want, and a greater chance for the fullest development of human capabilities.

32. Marcuse. *An Essay on Liberation.* Boston: Beacon Press, 1969, p. 90.

33. Marcuse. *Counter-Revolution and Revolt.* Boston: Beacon Press, 1972, p. 16.

34. Marcuse. *An Essay on Liberation*, pp. 23–24.

35. Marcuse. *Eros and Civilization*, pp. 162–164.

36. *Ibid.*, p. 166.

37. Marcuse. *Counter-Revolution and Revolt*, p. 69.

38. Marcuse. *Eros and Civilization*, p. 231.

39. *Ibid.*, p. 232.

40. *Ibid.*, pp. 140–141.

41. *Ibid.*, p. 142.

42. *Ibid.*, p. 144.

43. Marcuse. *Eros and Civilization*, pp. 174–177.

44. *Ibid.*, pp. 185–191.

45. *Ibid.*, p. 188.

46. *Ibid.*, p. 192.

47. Marcuse. *An Essay on Liberation*, p. 53.

48. *Ibid.*, p. 38.

49. Marcuse. *The Aesthetic Dimension*, p.16.

50. Marcuse. *Eros and Civilization*, p. 145.

51. Marcuse. *The Aesthetic Dimension*, p. 69.

52. *Ibid.*, pp. 32–33. This emphasis on needs and sensibilities resulted from his conviction that the proletariat no longer represents the determinate negation of society. In an attempt to identify the possible catalysts of revolutionary change, he turned his attention to various outgroups such as students, women, the poor and third world minorities. In the end, however, he concluded that the subject to which authentic art might appeal "is socially anonymous; it does not coincide with the potential subject of revolutionary practice." *Ibid.*

53. Marcuse. *The Aesthetic Dimension*, pp. 68–72.

54. *Ibid.*, p. 73.

Chapter 3

1. Rawls discussed the contrast between the "liberties of the moderns and the liberties of the ancients" in "Kantian Constructivism in Moral Theory." *Journal of Philosophy* 77 (Sept.

1980), pp. 519–522. The priority of the right is central to his theory of justice as fairness.

2. See John Rawls. *A Theory of Justice.* Cambridge: Harvard University Press, 1971 and *Political Liberalism.* New York: Columbia University Press, 1993. For a recent study of Rawls's philosophy, see *The Cambridge Companion to Rawls,* Ed. Samuel Freeman. Cambridge: Cambridge University Press, 2003.

3. Aristotle. *The Politics,* 1324a5–8 and 1325b15–17. *The Works of Aristotle.* Ed. W.D. Ross. Oxford: Clarenden Press, 1926, pp. 24–25 and 30–32.

4. Plato. *The Republic,* Book III, 414A–415E, *Great Dialogues of Plato.* Trans. W.H.D. Rouse. New York: Mentor Books, 1956, p. 215.

5. Aristotle. *The Politics,* 1325b2–5. Ed. Stephen Everson. Cambridge: Cambridge University Press, 1988, p. 161.

6. John Stuart Mill. *On Liberty* (1859). Ed. Elizabeth Rapaport. Indianapolis: Hackett, 1978, p. 12.

7. Mill noted that: "It is accordingly on this battleground, almost solely, that the rights of the individual against society have been asserted on broad grounds of principle, and the claim of society to exercise authority over dissentients openly controverted." *Ibid.,* p. 7.

8. *Ibid.,* p. 9. For Mill, harm to others includes the harm caused by acts and by failures to act. In his view, the failure to pay one's taxes constitutes a harm to others which society has the right to punish. This conception of harm suggests that persons possess not only the negative right to be free from interference, but the positive right to share in the goods of society.

9. *Ibid.,* pp. 53 ff.

10. Thomas Hobbes. *Leviathan* (1651). Ed. Michael Oakeshott. New York: Macmillan, 1962. For an analysis of Hobbes's psychological theory, see pp. 21–55.

11. *Ibid.,* p. 132.

12. John Locke. *Second Treatise of Government* (1690). Ed. C.B. Macpherson. Indianapolis: Hackett, 1980, p. 70.

13. Macpherson has pointed out the ambiguity in Locke's use of a state of nature. He contends that while Locke believed humans to be reasonable enough to honor their promises, they are not so reasonable that they can do without a mechanism to enforce promises that are not kept. Locke's theory provides for both a delegation and a retention of powers by the people, making possible the right of revolution. Locke's theory of a partial delegation of powers to the sovereign reveals an ambivalence about human nature. According to Locke, human beings desire happiness and generally know how to go about finding it. However, the state is necessary to protect us from those who would violate our right to the pursuit of happiness. Because protecting property was broadly construed in Locke's time, it was thought that the right to property was tantamount to protecting the right to pursue happiness. Cf. C.B. Macpherson. "Editor's Introduction." *Second Treatise of Government,* pp. vii–xxi and Leonard W. Levy. "Property as a Human Right." *Constitutional Commentary* 5 (1988), pp. 169–84. See also Macpherson. *The Political Theory of Possessive Individualism.* Oxford: Oxford University Press, 1964.

14. Locke. *Two Treatises of Government,* Sects. 123, 173. Ed. Peter Laslett. Cambridge: Cambridge University Press, 1963, cited in Levy, p. 175, n.27.

15. For Locke, our right to property is derived from our equal right to life. But the equal right to property in the state of nature is altered by the invention of money. Because money solves

the problem of spoilage, it is permissible, according to Locke, for a person to own more than he can consume. Private ownership is acceptable even where there is not enough left over for others because it is presumed that such ownership contributes to the wealth of society and, thereby, promotes the general welfare. This rationale suggests that citizens in advanced industrial society may possess a Lockean right to livelihood.

16. 1 J. Locke, 348, 355 (A. Fraser ed. 1894) cited in Levy at 172, n.11. See also 2 id. at Ch. XXI.

17. Locke. *Second Treatise of Government*, p. 52.

18. Jean Jacques Rousseau. *On the Social Contract* (1726). Trans. and ed. Donald Cress. Indianapolis: Hackett, 1987, p. 24.

19. *Ibid.*

20. *Ibid.*, p. 27.

21. *Ibid.*, p. 46.

22. For the classic account of the contrast between positive and negative freedom, see Isiah Berlin. *Four Essays on Liberty.* London: Oxford University Press, 1969.

23. Dworkin's focus on the right to equal concern and respect is largely compatible with Rawls's two principles of justice. Both emphasize the importance of individual liberty and both take the social bases of self-respect to be essential to social justice.

24. Robert Nozick. *Anarchy, State and Utopia.* New York: Basic Books, 1974.

25. Rawls. *A Theory of Justice.* Cambridge: Harvard University Press, 1971, p. 24.

26. Henry Sidgwick. *The Methods of Ethics.* London: Macmillan, 1907, p. 382.

27. Actually this identification is somewhat misleading because it ignores differences within utilitarian theory between hedonistic and ideal conceptions of the good and between egoistic and altruistic frames of reference. I do not claim that classical utilitarians agree on the nature of the good, only that they believe that such a good exists. Hedonists, for example, believe that pleasure is the only good while ideal utilitarians consider beauty or knowledge intrinsically good. Mill tried to rank various pleasures as higher and lower. The inherent difficulty of such an endeavor contributed to the development of preference utilitarianism.

28. Rawls. *A Theory of Justice*, p. 28.

29. *Ibid.*, p. 24.

30. *Ibid.*, pp. 26–27.

31. Ibid., p. 31.

32. *Ibid.*, p. 33.

33. *Ibid.*, p. 233.

34. *Ibid.*, p. 246.

35. Of course, Rawls did not seek to simply maximize liberty because to do would undermine our interest in equality.

36. Rawls. *A Theory of Justice*, p. 447.

37. *Ibid.*, pp. 447–448

38. *Ibid.*, pp. 448–449.

39. For Marx, self-development meant the free and full development of the abilities of each person. See *The German Ideology. Collected Works*, Vol 5. New York: International Publishers, 1976, pp. 224–225. Conceived in this way, a society which makes it possible for

each person to freely develop his talents and abilities would not violate its principles in trading off one person's good for another's. Here, the free and full development of human abilities provides a complement to Rawls's conception of the just society as the one which provides the greatest equal liberty. If Marx is right about human nature, then a society which provides the greatest equal liberty would also be the one in which human beings freely develop their abilities to the greatest extent possible.

40. Marx is commonly associated with such goals, but his repeated criticism of the language of rights and justice, and the historical experience of socialist societies, has led some to conclude that individual rights are incompatible with socialism. While Marx's position on the subject of justice is uncertain, it is clear that he was not a utilitarian. Nor did Marx believe that anything was justified if it promoted the goal of socialism. His antipathy to rights talk may have been due to the ideological role such language played in justifying capitalism. For a discussion of Marx and theories of justice, see Richard Miller. *Analyzing Marx*. Princeton: Princeton University Press, 1984, chapters 1 and 2 and Kai Nielsen. *Marxism and the Moral Point of View*. Boulder: Westview Press, 1989.

41. Will Kymlicka. "Rawls on Teleology and Deontology." *Philosophy and Public Affairs* 17, (Summer 1988), pp. 173–190. See also, Kynlicka. *Contemporary Political Philosophy*. Oxford, New York: Oxford University Press, 2002, pp. 53–96.

42. *Ibid.*, p. 173. Kymlicka believed that only fascists and immoralists believe that the social good should be maximized without giving equal consideration to each person's good. For utilitarianism, giving equal consideration means counting each person's preference for one and no one's preference for more than one. Kymlicka argued that Rawls's distinction between teleological and deontological theories is based on a confusion of two issues, neither of which concerns the priority of the right or the good. One issue involves the definition of our essential interests. The other concerns principles of distribution which follow from supposing that our interests matter equally.

43. *Ibid.*, p. 175. Ronald Dworkin endorsed affirmative action on essentially utilitarian grounds because in promoting greater social equality the policy treats individuals with equal concern and respect. See Dworkin. "Why Bakke Has No Case." *New York Review of Books 24*, No. 18, November 10, 1977.

44. *Ibid.*, p. 177.

45. *Ibid.*, p. 184.

46. Rawls. "Reply to Alexander and Musgrave." *Quarterly Journal of Economics* 53 (1974), p. 641, cited in Kymlicka. "Rawls on Teleology and Deontology," p. 186, note 19.

47. Kymlicka. *Ibid.*, p. 187.

48. *Ibid.*

49. Another way of conceiving a common good was described by Gerald Postema in "Collective Evils, Harms, and the Law." *Ethics* 97 (1987), pp. 414–440. He described collective goods as things which "express and depend essentially upon shared meaning, understandings, and valuings which are not just convergent, but common and interdependent." *Id.* at 425. Such goods include the preservation of the wilderness, our cultural heritage, and a distinctive city ambience of parks and monuments. See also, Joel Feinberg. *Harmless Wrongdoing*. New York: Oxford University Press, 1988, pp. 33–37.

50. According to Gilligan: "When one begins with the study of women and derives develop-

mental constructs from their lives, the outline of a moral conception. . . begins to emerge.
. . In this conception, the moral problem arises from conflicting responsibilities rather than
from competing rights and requires for its resolution a mode of thinking that is contextual
and narrative rather than formal and abstract. *In a Different Voice*. Cambridge: Harvard
University Press, 1982, p. 19.

51. Annette Baier. "Hume, the Women's Moral Theorist?" *Women and Moral Theory*. Ed. Eva
Feder Kittay and Diana T. Meyers. Totowa, N.J.: Rowman and Littlefield, 1987, pp. 44–45.

52. Duncan Kennedy. "Form and Substance in Private Law Adjudication." *Harvard Law Review*
89 (1976), pp. 1685–1778.

53. Roberto Unger. *The Critical Legal Studies Movement*. Cambridge: Harvard University
Press, 1986, p. 51. In response to Unger's assertions, Andrew Altman wrote that in a
pluralist society principles such as equal protection will be necessarily truncated. See
Altman. *Critical Legal Studies: A Liberal Critique*. Princeton: Princeton University Press,
1990, pp. 86 ff.

54. Alisdair MacIntyre. *After Virtue*. Notre Dame: Notre Dame University Press, 1981, pp.
204–205.

55. *A Theory of Justice*, pp. 310–315. Rawls rejected desert as a basis for distributional justice
because the distribution of natural talents is morally arbitrary.

Chapter 4

1. John Rawls. *A Theory of Justice*, p. 28.

2. *Ibid.*, p. 29.

3. *Ibid.*, p. 447.

4. In response to criticism that his list of social primary goods is overly materialistic, Rawls
later acknowledged that the list could be expanded to include goods such as leisure time and
the absence of physical pain. See Rawls. "The Priority of Right and the Ideas of the Good."
Philosophy and Public Affairs, (Fall, 1988), p. 257.

5. *A Theory of Justice,* p. 396.

6. *Ibid.*, p. 127.

7. *Ibid.*, p. 129.

8. Rawls. "Justice as Fairness: Political not Metaphysical." *Philosophy and Public Affairs,*
(Summer 1985), pp. 223-251 and "The Idea of an Overlapping Consensus." *Oxford Journal
of Legal Studies,* (Spring 1987), pp. 1–27.

9. Rawls. *A Theory of Justice*, p. 302.

10. *Ibid.*

11. *Ibid.,* p. 62.

12. *Ibid.*, p. 440.

13. *Ibid.*, pp. 152 ff.

14. *Ibid.*, p. 302. For a critical analysis of the plausibility of the maximin strategy, see R.M.
Hare. "Rawls' Theory of Justice." *Reading Rawls*. Ed. Norman Daniels.. New York: Basic
Books, 1974, pp. 102–107 and Richard Miller. "Rights and Reality." *Philosophical Review*
40, 1981, pp. 383–407. Both authors reject the strategy as dependent on an implausible
characterization of human beings as risk-averse. Instead, they believe that rational con-

tractors might easily endorse a system maximizing average utility along with a social minimum.

15. *Ibid.*, p. 302.
16. *Ibid.*, p. 560.
17. *Ibid.*, pp. 118 ff.
18. *Ibid.*, pp. 152 ff.
19. Michael J. Sandel. *Liberalism and the Limits of Justice.*New York: Cambridge University Press, 1982, p. 59.
20. *Ibid.*, p. 21.
21. *Ibid.*, p. 22.
22. *Ibid.*, pp. 52–53.
23. Although Rawls did not describe happiness as a dominant end, he wrote on page 548 of *A Theory of Justice* that "a person is happy when he is in the way of a successful execution (more or less) of a rational plan of life drawn up under (more or less) favorable conditions, and he is reasonably confident that his intentions can be carried through." Thus, it would be fair to say that the social primary goods and the principles of justice are adopted in order to allow persons to increase the likelihood of happiness.
24. Rawls. *A Theory of Justice*, p. 315.
25. *Ibid.*, pp. 66–70.
26. Although it may be possible to satisfy the least advantaged group in some situations with the payment of compensation, the amount of compensation needed would make this option extremely burdensome in many cases. Where the goods involved are incommensurable as is the case in the dispute over the development of our forests, it is unlikely that any amount of compensation would satisfy those opposed to development.
27. Rawls. *A Theory of Justice*, pp. 83–89.
28. See Mark Sagoff. "Economic Theory and Environmental Law." 79 *Mich. Law Rev.*, pp. 1393, 1411–1412 (1981). Sagoff wrote that: "Private and public preferences also belong to different logical categories. Public preferences do not involve desires or wants, but opinions or beliefs. They state what a person believes is best or right for the community or group as a whole…. [A]n economist who asks how much citizens would pay for opinions that they advocate through political association commits a category-mistake. The economist asks of objective beliefs a question that is appropriate only to subjective wants."
29. In *Happiness: Lessons From a New* Science. New York: The Penguin Press, 2005, Richard Layard made a convincing argument the increases in income wealth in the developed world over the past 50 years have not produced any measurable increase in human happiness.
30. Robert Nozick. *Anarchy, State and Utopia.*
31. *Ibid.,* p. 170.
32. MacIntyre, *After Virtue*, pp. 221 ff.
33. *Ibid.*, p. 229.
34. Rawls. *A Theory of Justice*, pp. 310–315.
35. Actually, Rawls believed that justice as fairness is compatible with both public and private ownership of the means of production. See *Ibid.*, pp. 210–274. However, by public ownership Rawls meant ownership by the state. In treating the state as a capitalist, he ignored the thrust of Marx's critique. What is objectionable about private ownership of the means

of production—alienated labor and social division—is not remedied by state ownership. In viewing persons as consumers rather than producers of value, Rawls underestimated the importance of workplace democracy. The alternative to private ownership is not state socialism, but economic democracy.

36. G.A. Cohen. "The Structure of Proletarian Unfreedom." *Philosophy and Public Affairs* 12, (Winter 1983), pp. 3–33.

37. Jeffrey Reiman. "Exploitation, Force, and the Moral Assessment of Capitalism: Thoughts on Roemer and Cohen." *Philosophy and Public Affairs* 16, (Winter, 1987), pp. 3–41.

38. *Ibid.*, p. 16.

39. I suggest that the wage relationship represents a false necessity because, while it is necessary that persons labor in order to satisfy their needs, it is not necessary that they alienate their labor in return for a wage. Worker-owned enterprises may be organized in a manner that permits a far greater measure of self-determination.

Chapter 5

1. G.A. Cohen. "Reconsidering Historical Materialism." *Labor, History and Freedom*. Oxford: Clarendon Press, 1988, pp. 137 ff.

2. *Ibid.*, p. 138.

3. *Ibid.*, p. 139.

4. *Ibid.*, p. 141.

5. *Ibid.*, note 13.

6. Karl Marx. "The German Ideology." *Collected Works*, Vol. 5. New York: International Publishers, 1976, p. 393.

7. *Ibid.*

8. *Ibid.*, p. 394.

9. Marx. *"The German Ideology."* The Marx-Engels Reader. Ed. Robert Tucker. New York: W.W. Norton, 1978, p. 160.

10. Cohen. "Reconsidering Historical Materialism," p. 143, note 17.

11. *Ibid.*, pp. 143–144

12. *Ibid.*, p. 142, note 15 citing *"The German Ideology."* Collected Works, Vol. 5, p. 225.

13. Marx. "The German Ideology." *Collected Works*, Vol. 5., pp. 224–225.

14. *Ibid.*, p. 225.

15. Cohen. "Reconsidering Historical Materialism," p. 142, note 16.

16. Marx. *"The German Ideology."Collected Works*, Vol. 5., pp. 255–256.

17. Marx. *"Economic and Philosophic Manuscripts of 1844."* The. Marx-Engels Reader, p. 74.

18. Cohen. "The Dialectic of Labour in Marx." *Labor, History and Freedom*, p. 206.

19. Cohen. "Reconsidering Historical Materialism," p. 143 quoting *The German Ideology. Collected Works*, Vol. 5., p. 78.

20. This claim should be qualified by Cohen's statement that: "I do not say that Marx denied that there is a need for self definition, but he failed to give the truth due emphasis, and Marxist tradition has followed his lead. *Ibid.*, p. 138. While it is reasonable to disagree over whether something is given the emphasis it is due, Marx clearly recognized the need for self definition and addressed this need throughout his philosophical anthropology.

21. Marx. "The German Ideology." *Collected Works*, Vol. 5, pp. 77–78.
22. Marx. *"Economic and Philosophic Manuscripts of 1844." The Marx-Engels Reader*, pp. 85–86.
23. Marx used the term exploitation to refer to the process by which surplus labor is extracted from the worker. Because the value of labor may exceed the value of the labor power for which the worker is paid, the wage will be less than the value the labor creates. Under the labor theory of value, it is possible to break up the work day into portions of labor necessary to reproduce the laborer and surplus labor which creates profit for the capitalist. For Marx, ending exploitation was not enough to overcome alienation. Even if workers had full control of their labor power, as would be the case under a system of simple commodity production, they would nevertheless feel alienated in a society where individuals are not regarded as sharing the same species being. In other words, what is alienated in pre-communist society is not simply our creative powers, but also our species being. Or, to phrase it differently, the free and full development of human powers must include the development of human solidarity made possible only with the emergence of communism.
24. Marx. Excerpt Notes of 1844. Writings of the Young Marx on Philosophy and Society. Ed.. Loyd Easton and Kurt Guddat. New York: Doubleday, 1967, pp. 278–279.
25. Cohen. "Reconsidering Historical Materialism," p. 138.
26. *Ibid.*, p. 139.
27. *Ibid.*, p. 144.
28. In making this case, it is important to distinguish self-identity from personal identity. The latter depends on a person's race, gender, religion, nationality, social role, personal history and individual characteristics. While these elements are central to personal identity, they are insufficient to frame a theory of the self.
29. Marx. *Economic and Philosophic Manuscripts of 1844. The Marx-Engels Reader*, p. 76.
30. Marx. *Capital*, Vol. 1. *The Marx-Engels Reader*, pp.144–145.
31. Marx. *"Theses on Feuerbach." The Marx-Engels Reader*, p.145.

Chapter 6

1. David Hume. *A Treatise of Human Nature* (1739). Ed. L.A. Selby-Bigge. Oxford: Oxford University Press, 1965.
2. *Ibid.*, Appendix A.
3. Daniel Flage. "Hume's Identity Crisis." *The Modern Schoolman*, LVIII, November, 1980, pp.21–35.
4. See D.T. Suzuki. *Essays in Zen Buddhism.* Boston: Beacon Press, 1952. For a discussion of the parallels in Eastern and Western thought, see Van Meter Ames. *Zen and American Thought.* Honolulu: University of Hawaii Press, 1962.
5. *Hegel. "The Phenomenology of the Spirit." The Philosophy of Hegel.* Ed. Carl Friedrich. New York: Random House, 1954, p. 410.
6. Edmund Husserl. *Author's Preface to the English Edition of Ideas.* Trans. W.R. Boyce Gibson, reprinted in *Husserl: Shorter Works.* Ed. Peter McCormick and Frederick Elliston. Notre Dame: University of Notre Dame Press, 1981, pp. 46–47.
7. Gottfried Leibnit. *The Monadology.* Trans. Robert Latta. London: Oxford University Press,

1971.

8. Fritjof Capra. *The Tao of Physics*. Boston: Shambhala, 2000.

9. *Ibid.*, pp. 68–69.

10. *Ibid.*, p. 24.

11. *Ibid.*, pp.. 299-300 citing G.F. Chew. "'Bootstrap': A Scientific Idea?" *Science*, Vol. 161 (May 23, 1968) p. 763.

12. *Ibid.*, p. 300.

13. *Ibid.*, pp. 61–62.

14. *Ibid.*, p. 170.

15. *Ibid.*, p. 178.

16. *Ibid.*, pp. 311–313. Instantaneous communication between subatomic particles may also provide an explanation for phenomena such as telepathy and clairvoyance. For a discussion of the relation of quantum physics to psychic phenomena see H.M. Collins and T.J. Pinch. *Frames of Meaning.* London: Routledge and Kegan Paul, 1982, pp. 66–99.

17. *Ibid.*, p. 247.

18. *Ibid*, pp. 77–80.

19. *Ibid.*, pp. 202–203.

20. *Ibid.*, pp. 222–223.

21. Deepak Chopra. *How to Know God.* New York: Harmony Books, 2000.

22. *Ibid.*, p. 280.

23. *Ibid.*

24. *Ibid.*, pp. 31–32.

25. *Ibid.*, p. 206.

26. *Ibid.*, p. 41.

27. *Ibid.*, p. 138.

28. *Ibid.*, p. 216.

29. *Ibid.*, p. 226.

30. *Ibid.*, p. 241.

31. *Ibid.*, p. 243.

32. *Ibid.*, p. 257.

33. Stephen Hawking. *A Brief History of Time.* New York: Bantam Books, 1998, p. 49.

34. *Ibid.*, p.129.

35. *Ibid.*, p.126.

36. See Raynor Johnson. *The Imprisoned Splendour.* Hodder and Stoughton, 1953 and *The Watcher on the Hill.* Hodder and Stoughton, 1959 cited in Mona Coxhood. *The Relevance of Bliss.* New York: St. Martin's Press, 1985, pp. 3–4.

37. See, for example, Duncan Kennedy. "Form and Substance in Private Law Adjudication." *Harvard Law Review* 89, 1976.

38. A similar question arises in relation to the claims of ethical egoism. Moral behavior is generally rationalized on prudential grounds. To the person who is convinced that immoral behavior will better promote his self-interest, however, all one can argue is that he may develop a character he will later regret. While this argument may deter some immorality, its appeal seems limited to those persons who are already concerned about developing a moral character. It will certainly not move the committed ethical egoist. From the per-

spective of a universal self, however, altruism and morality are perfectly natural. One need not rely on prudential arguments for either ideal.

39. John-Paul Sartre. *Nausea.* New York: New Directions Publishing Corp., 1964, p. 126.

40. *Ibid.*, pp. 127–134.

41. *Ibid.*, p. 135.

42. Walt Whitman. "Song of Myself," *Leaves of Grass.* Ed. Sculley Bradley and Harold Blodgett. New York: H. H. Norton and Co. 1973, pp. 80–88.

Chapter 7

1. Hume reached the same conclusion when he distinguished natural virtues such as benevolence from artificial ones like justice. Hume believed that justice was an artificial virtue which could be dispensed with in a world in which perfect benevolence was practiced. See David Hume. *An Enquiry Concerning the Principles of Morals* (1717). La Salle, IL: Open Court, 1933, pp. 8–21.

2. Richard Layard. *Happiness: Lessons From a New* Science. New York: The Penguin Press, 2005, pp. 41 ff.

3. *Ibid.,* pp. 62 ff.

4. *Ibid., pp.* 223 ff.

5. Michael Tooley. "Abortion and Infanticide." *Applied Ethics.* Ed. Peter Singer. Oxford: Oxford University Press, 1986.

6. *Ibid.*, p. 85.

7. Peter Singer. "All Animals Are Equal." *Applied Ethics*, p. 221, quoting Bentham.

Bibliography

Adorno, Theodore. "Freudian Theory and the Pattern of Fascist Propaganda." *The Essential Frankfurt School Reader*. Ed. Andrew Arato and Eike Gebhardt. New York: Continuum, 1982.

Altman, Andrew. *Critical Legal Studies: A Liberal Critique*. Princeton: Princeton University Press, 1990.

Ames, Van Meter. *Zen and American Thought*. Honolulu: University of Hawaii Press, 1962.

Aristotle. *The Works of Aristotle*. Ed. W. D. Ross. Oxford: Clarenden Press, 1926.

_____. *The Politics*. Ed. Stephen Everson. Cambridge: Cambridge University Press, 1988.

Baier, Anette. "Hume, the Women's Moral Theorist?" *Women and Moral Theory*. Ed. Eva Feder Kittay and Diana T. Meyers. Totowa, N.J.: Rowman and Littlefield, 1987.

Berlin, Isiah. *Four Essays on Liberty*. London: Oxford University Press, 1969.

Capra, Fritjof. *The Tao of Physics*. Boston: Shambhala, 2000.

Chopra, Deepak. *How to Know God. New York:* Harmony Books, 2000.

Cohen, G.A. *Labor, History and Freedom*. Oxford: Clarendon Press, 1988.

_____. 'The Structure of Proletarian Unfreedom' in *Philosophy and Public Affairs* 12, Winter 1983.

Collins, H. M. and Pinch, T.J. Frames of Meaning. London: Routledge and Kegan Paul, 1982.

Coxhood, Mona. *The Relevance of Bliss*. New York: St. Martin's Press, 1985.

Diogenes Laertius. *Lives of Eminent Philosophers*. Trans. R. D. Hicks. New York: Putnam, New York, 1925.

Dworkin, Ronald. "Why Bakke Has No Case." *New York Review of Books 24*, No. 18, November 10, 1977.

Feinberg, Joel. *Harmless Wrongdoing*. New York: Oxford University Press, 1988.

Flage, Daniel. "Hume's Identity Crisis."*The Modern Schoolman*, LVIII, November, 1980.

Freeman, Samuel. Ed. *The Cambridge Companion to Rawls*. Cambridge: Cambridge University Press, 2003.

Freud, Sigmund. *Beyond the Pleasure Principle*. Trans. and ed. James Strachey, New York: Liveright, 1961.

_____. *Civilization and its Discontents*. Trans. and ed. James Strachey. New York: W.W. Norton, 1962.

_____. *Group Psychology and the Analysis of the Ego*. London: The International Psychoanalytical Press, 1922.

Gilligan, Carol. *In a Different Voice*. Cambridge: Harvard University Press, 1982.

Hare, R. M. "Rawls' Theory of Justice." *Reading Rawls*. Ed. Norman Daniels. New York: Basic Books.

Hawking, Stephen. *A Brief History of Time. New York:* Bantam Books, 1998.

Hegel, Georg. *The Phenomenology of the Spirit.The Philosophy of Hegel*. Ed. Carl Friedrich. New York: Random House, 1954.

Hobbes, Thomas. *Leviathan*. Ed. Michael Oakeshott. New York: Macmillan, 1962.

Hume, David.. *A Treatise of Human Nature* (1739). Ed. L.A. Selby-Bigge. Oxford: Oxford University Press, 1965.

_____. An Enquiry Concerning the Principles of Morals, LaSalle, IL: Open Court, 1933.

Husserl, Edmund. "Author's Preface to the English Edition of Ideas." Trans. W. R. Boyce Gibson. *Husserl: Shorter Works*. Ed. Peter McCormick and Frederick Elliston, Notre Dame, IN: University of Notre Dame Press, 1981.

Johnson, R., *The Imprisoned Splendour*. London: Hodder and Stoughton, 1953.

_____. *The Watcher on the Hill*. London: Hodder and Stoughton, 1959.

Kennedy, Duncan. "Form and Substance in Private Law Adjudication."*Harvard Law Review* 89 (1976).

Kymlicka, Will. "Rawls on Teleology and Deontology." *Philosophy and Public Affairs* 17, Summer 1988.

_____. *Contemporary Political Philosophy*. Oxford, New York: Oxford University Press, 2002.

Layard, Richard. *Happiness: Lessons from a New Science*. New York: The Penguin Press, 2005.

Leibnitz, Gottfried. *The Monadology*. Trans. Robert Latta. London: Oxford University Press, 1971.

Levy, Leonard. "Property as a Human Right." *Constitutional Commentary* 5, 1988.

Locke, John. *Second Treatise of Government*. Ed. C.B. Macpherson. Indianapolis: Hackett, 1980.

_____. *Two Treatises of Government*. Ed. Peter Laslett, Cambridge: Cambridge University Press, 1963.

MacIntyre, Alasdair. *After Virtue*. Notre Dame, IN: Notre Dame University Press, 1981.

Macpherson, C.B., *The Political Theory of Possessive Individualism*. Oxford: Oxford University Press, 1964.

Marcuse, Herbert. *An Essay on Liberation*. Boston: Beacon Press, 1969.

_____. *Counter-Revolution and Revolt*. Boston: Beacon Press, 1972.

_____. *Eros and Civilization*. Boston: Beacon Press, 1966.

_____. *From Luther to Popper*. London: Verso, 1983.

_____. *Negation*. Trans. Jeremy Shapiro. Boston: Beacon Press, 1968.

_____. *One-Dimensional Man*. Boston: Beacon Press, 1964.

_____. *Reason and Revolution*. London: Routledge and Kegan, 1969.

_____. "Some Social Implications of Modern Technology." *The Essential Frankfurt School Reader*. Ed. Andrew Arato and Eike Gebhardt. New York: Continuum, 1982.

_____. *The Aesthetic Dimension*. Boston: Beacon Press, 1978.

Marx, Karl. *Capital*, Volume I. Ed. Ben Fowkes. New York: New York: Vintage Books, 1977.

_____. *Economic and Philosophical Manuscripts of 1844*. London: Lawrence and Wisehart, 1970.

_____. *The German Ideology. Collected Works*, Volume 5. New York: International Publishers, 1976.

_____. *The German Ideology* and *Thesis on Feuerbach. The Marx-Engels Reader*. Ed. Robert Tucker. New York: W.W. Norton, 1978.

_____. *Excerpt-Notes of 1844* and *Thesis on Feuerbach. Writings of the Young Marx on Philosophy and Society*. Trans. and Ed. Loyd Easton and Kurt Guddatt. Garden City, New York:

Doubleday, 1967.

McGill, V.J. *The Idea of Happiness*. New York: Edward A. Praeger, 1967.

Mill, John Stuart. *On Liberty*., Ed. Elizabeth Rapaport. Indianapolis: Hackett, 1978.

Miller, Richard. *Analyzing Marx*. Princeton: Princeton University Press, 1984.

_____. "Rights and Reality." *Philosophical Review* 40, 1981.

Nielsen, Kai., *Marxism and the Moral Point of View* . Boulder: Westview,1989.

Nietzsche, Freidrich. *The Birth of Tragedy*. Trans. Walter Kaufmann. New York: Random House, 1967.

Nozick, Robert. *Anarchy, State and Utopia*. New York: Basic Books, 1974.

Plato, *Great Dialogues of Plato*. Trans. W.H.D. Rouse. New York: Mentor Books, 1956.

_____. *The* Republic, Ttrans. Benjamin Jowett. Buffalo: Prometheus, 1986.

_____. Phaedrus. Ttrans. R. Hackforth. New York: The Liberal Arts Press, 1952.

Postema, Gerald. " Collective Evils, Harms, and the Law." *Ethics* 97, 1987.

Rawls, *John. A Theory of Justice*. Cambridge: Harvard University Press, 1971.

_____. "Justice as Fairness: Political not Metaphysical." *Philosophy and Public Affairs* 14 , Summer 1985.

_____. "Kantian Constructivism in Moral Theory." *Journal of Philosophy* 77, Sept. 1980.

_____. *Political Liberalism*..New York: Columbia University Press, 1993.

_____. "Reply to Alexander and Musgrave."*Quarterly Journal of Economics* 53, 1974.

_____. "The Idea of an Overlapping Consensus." *Oxford Journal of Legal Studies* 7, Spring 1987.

_____. 'The Priority of Right and the Ideas of the Good." *Philosophy and Public Affairs*, Fall 1988.

Reiman, Jeffrey. "Exploitation, Force, and the Moral Assessment of Capitalism: Thoughts on Roemer and Cohen." *Philosophy and Public Affairs* 16, Winter, 1987.

Rousseau, Jean-Jacques. *On the Social Contract*. Trans. and ed. Donald Cress. Indianapolis: Hackett, 1987.

Sagoff, Mark. "Economic Theory and Environmental Law."79 *Mich. Law Rev*., No. 7, June 1981.

Sandel, Michael J. *Liberalism and the Limits of Justice*. New York: Cambridge University Press, 1982.

Sartre, Jean-Paul. *Nausea*. New York: New Directions, 1964.

Singer, Peter. "All Animals Are Equal." *Applied Ethics*. Ed. Peter Singer. Oxford: Oxford University Press, 1986.

Sidgwick, Henry. *The Methods of Ethics*. London: Macmillan, 1907.

Suzuki, D.T. *Essays in Zen Buddhism*. Boston: Beacon Press, 1952.

Tooley, Michael. "Abortion and Infanticide."'*Applied Ethics*. Ed. Peter Singer. Oxford: Oxford University Press, 1986.

Unger, Roberto. *The Critical Legal Studies Movement*. Cambridge: Harvard University Press, 1986.

Whitman, Walt. *Leaves of Grass*. Ed. Sculley Bradley and Harold Blodgett. New York: H. H. Norton, 1973.